ON YAMAHA
Street Bikes

1970-1974

Reprinted From
Cycle World Magazine

ISBN 1 869826 949

Published By
Brooklands Books with permission of Cycle World

Titles in this series

Distributed By

Cycle World
1499 Monrovia Avenue
Newport Beach
California 92663 U.S.A.

Brooklands Book Distribution Ltd.
Holmerise, Seven Hills Road,
Cobham, Surrey KT11 1ES,
England

CYCLE WORLD

We are frequently asked for copies of out of print Road Tests and other articles that have appeared in Cycle World. To satisfy this need we are producing a series of books that will include, as nearly as possible, all the important information on one make or subject for a given period.

It is our hope that these collections of articles will give an overview that will be of value to historians, restorers and potential buyers, as well as to present owners of these interesting motorcycles.

Printed in Hong Kong

YAMAHA XS-650

Breaking With Tradition To Extend
An Older One, Yamaha Comes Up
With A Well-Disguised Racing
Engine In A Sporting Big
Bore Roadster.

CYCLE WORLD
ROAD TEST

YAMAHA'S NEW BIG BORE will be likely to cause confusion to innocent bystanders. From a distance it resembles several other machines that follow the almost-classic 650-cc or 750-cc vertical Twin pattern.

It may seem strange that Yamaha—breaking with tradition to build its first four-stroke machine—would follow a path already beaten. Starting from scratch they could have opted to build a three- or four-cylinder super bike. But the situation in both the Japanese and U.S. markets made the 650 Twin a wiser choice. For one thing, the big domestic market in Japan is becoming more affluent. Like many Americans, they buy up the medium displacement machines in great droves, but hanker after that day when they can own a "real" (translate that as

"big displacement") motorcycle. The jump in cost and size, from a 250 or 350, to a 650 Twin, is not quite so big as to a larger one. Expanding markets in S.E. Asia are also getting ripe for a 650. In the U.S., where the superbike battle is raging, the XS-650 slips neatly into that less costly "in-between" area.

It's not a bad move, as the vertical Twin has been a popularly accepted form of sporting transportation in the U.S. for about two decades. As a design, it is pre-sold. It is reasonably compact and light, and lends itself to sporting applications, both in everyday road use and on the race track.

There is no question that Yamaha has achieved the classic Big Twin "feel." Start the XS-650, sit on it and close your eyes and you could be sitting on any one of four British

Twins. Seating position, handlebars, height, general balance and weight distribution, even the sound of the 360-degree alternate firing crankshaft arrangement, recall another country and a tradition other than Japanese.

But there are differences that are quite Japanese. Flywheel effect is lighter, and the engine picks up revs quite rapidly when the throttle is blipped. The five-speed gearbox shifts on the left. The XS-650 is delivered in a tractable state of tune, and doesn't really need the five ratios. But the gearbox, the single overhead camshaft, and the overall construction of the engine beg the race tuner's hand. The machine is robust, laid out for rapid access to its internals, and ready to be stretched.

It may seem rather rude to call the engine layout of the XS-650 "conventional," for the machine is the most sophisticated 650-cc Twin commercially produced. But conventional it is, in Japanese terms. And this normalcy is actually a desirable attribute. The practice is already proven.

For example, the crankcases split horizontally, offering the advantages of oil tightness through the elimination of vertical joints and one-step access to both the lower end and the gearbox. The 650's four-main-bearing crankshaft, made up of four separate flywheels, recalls the practice established by Honda in its smaller Twins. Couching that great rotating mass in so many main bearings virtually eliminates that old parallel Twin bugaboo—crankshaft flexure at high rpm. This may seem unnecessary in a machine with a 7000-rpm power peak, but it should be evident that the machine can be turned much tighter with safety. This leaves much room for annual development of production models, as well as any optional power kitting. And it should make Yamaha's active racing department mighty happy.

Alternate 360-degree firing order is used, giving even firing impulses, and that familiar husky sound that has been the trademark of the big Twins for years. A splined hub, connecting the two sets of flywheels, incorporates a sprocket to drive the overhead camshaft chain.

Rolling bearings are used throughout the engine. The timing side and the two center mains employ roller bearings, while the drive side is a ball bearing. The connecting rods use caged rollers at the big end, while caged needles are used for the wrist pins.

Aluminum pistons, slightly domed with valve pockets, are of three-ring design, with two compression rings and one oil control ring. The alloy cylinder barrel has iron liners. Ribs are cast between the fins to reduce the mechanical noise level. Noise suppression is also provided in the aluminum cylinder head by small white rubber discs placed alternately between the fins. These measures work quite effectively, counteracting the inherent sound transmitting nature of aluminum.

A spring loaded guide, attached to the wall of a cavity in the cylinder block, locates the cam drive chain, and takes up unnecessary slack. Chain tension is regulated by an external adjuster found at the rear of the cylinder. Full-length studs, originating in the top crankcase half, connect the entire head and cylinder assembly rigidly to the crankcases.

Oil pressure is provided by a gear pump driven by a steel spur gear off the crankshaft. The pump is in the primary drive cavity, on the right side of the engine. A double filtering process is incorporated in the lubrication cycle. Oil, passing through a screen at the bottom of the sump, circulates through the pump, and out through yet another screen before it is fed through both ends of the crankshaft to the big ends. Splash and oil mist lubricate the main bearings and wrist pin needles. Oil thrown from the connecting rod big ends is thrown onto the cylinder wall for additional lubrication of the piston skirts. Camshaft and rocker arms are pressure-fed by passageways

from an external oil tube at the front of the cylinder. Oil also feeds to the critical scuffing areas of the cam lobes and rockers. After draining down to the sump cavity, the oil begins a new cycle.

The overhead camshaft rides on four ball bearings. These bearings are narrow, two of them at each end of the cam.

Doubling up two narrow bearings increases load capacity over a single wide bearing of equivalent size.

Cam profile might be described as sporting but gentle, particularly for a "single knocker." Intake opens 47 degrees btc, closes 67 degrees abc; exhaust opens 60 bbc, and closes 41 atc, yielding intake duration of 294 degrees, exhaust duration

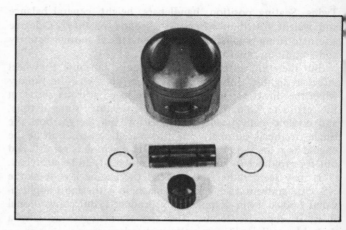

YAMAHA XS-650

SPECIFICATIONS

List price	$1245 p.o.e. West Coast
Suspension, front	telescopic fork
Suspension, rear	swinging arm
Tire, front	3.25-19
Tire, rear	4.00-18
Brake, front, diameter x width, in.	7.8 x 1.3
Brake, rear, diameter x width, in.	7.1 x 1.1
Total brake swept area, sq. in.	56.4
Brake loading, lb./sq. in.	10.5
Engine, type	sohc vertical Twin
Bore x stroke, in., mm	2.96 x 2.91, 75 x 74
Piston displacement, cu. in., cc	39.8, 654
Compression ratio	8.8:1
Carburetion	(2) Mikuni CV 30 mm
Ignition	battery-coil
Claimed bhp @ rpm	53 @ 7000
Oil system	wet sump
Oil capacity, pt.	6.0
Fuel capacity, U.S. gal.	3.3
Recommended fuel	premium
Starting system	kick, folding crank
Lighting system	12-V alternator
Air filtration	dry paper
Clutch	multi-disc, wet
Primary drive	gear
Final drive	5/8-in. x 3/8-in. chain
Gear ratios, overall:1	
5th	5.10
4th	5.83
3rd	6.95
2nd	8.45
1st	11.80
Wheelbase, in.	56.1
Seat height, in.	31.8
Seat width, in.	11.0
Handlebar width, in.	29.8
Footpeg height, in.	9.8
Ground clearance, in.	6.1
Curb weight (w/half-tank fuel), lb.	428
Weight bias, front/rear, percent	45/55
Test weight (fuel and rider), lb.	593

TEST CONDITIONS

Air temperature, degrees F	71
Humidity, percent	47
Barometric pressure, in. hg.	29.80
Altitude above mean sea level, ft.	350
Wind velocity, mph	3-5
Strip alignment, relative wind:	

WIND
S ⟶ F

PERFORMANCE

Top speed (actual @ 7220 rpm), mph	104.93
Computed top speed in gears (@ 7500 rpm), mph:	
5th	108
4th	98
3rd	82
2nd	67
1st	48
Mph/1000 rpm, top gear	14.39
Engine revolution/mile, top gear	4040
Piston speed (@ 7500 rpm), ft./min.	3635
Fuel consumption, mpg	44
Speedometer error:	
50 mph indicated, actually	45.91
60 mph indicated, actually	54.85
70 mph indicated, actually	64.70
Braking distance:	
from 30 mph, ft.	39
from 60 mph, ft.	127
Acceleration, zero to:	
30 mph, sec.	2.8
40 mph, sec.	3.2
50 mph, sec.	4.2
60 mph, sec.	5.4
70 mph, sec.	7.5
80 mph, sec.	9.9
90 mph, sec.	13.1
100 mph, sec.	21.0
Standing one-eighth mile, sec.	9.29
terminal speed, mph	79.08
Standing one-quarter mile, sec.	14.23
terminal speed, mph	93.26

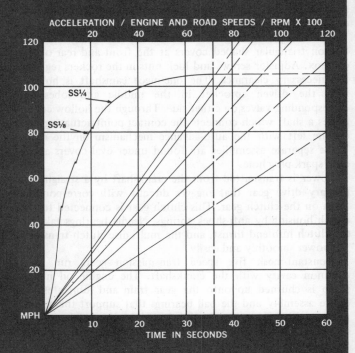

ACCELERATION / ENGINE AND ROAD SPEEDS / RPM X 100

TIME IN SECONDS

of 281, and overlap of 88. But the ramping to peak lift of .360 in. is mild. Presumably the upper power range of this machine, now limited to a 7500-rpm redline, would respond quite well to a hairier grind, and, as the 650 is obviously designed to stand higher rpm, this would be a likely place for the tuner to extract latent bhp.

On top of the head is a removable aluminum casting which carries the four individual rocker shafts; it doubles as the top half of the cambox. When this cover is removed, access to the cam and valve train is possible. The four valves are held on their seats by a pair of inner and outer coil springs. The spring retainers and keepers are steel. Automotive style umbrella type rubber oil seals slip over the valve stems, and form a barrier around the end of the guide to keep excess oil from seeping down into the intake and exhaust ports.

Valve adjustment gear is reached by removing the four bolt-on triangular shaped covers at the front and rear of the cambox. Adjuster screws and lock nuts in the rockers regulate the necessary clearance. The one-piece camshaft is hollow, with the driven sprocket in the middle and lobes for corresponding valves on either side. Through the hollow center passes a shaft which connects the contact point actuating cam on the left with the auto-advance mechanism on the right. These separate assemblies are found under oval covers above each spark plug hole.

Power is transmitted from the crankshaft by a straight-cut primary drive gear that engages directly with corresponding teeth on the clutch gear. This clutch gear is connected to the clutch housing by anti-shock springs. Needle bearings take up the clutch hub end thrust, and the multi-disc clutch transmits the power smoothly and easily.

Constant-mesh five speed transmission gears run in a common cavity with the crankshaft. The engine oil in the sump is churned up onto the gear train and lubricates the entire assembly and the ball bearings that support them. The primary drive gears are also lubricated by this method. With one source of lubrication taking care of everything, routine maintenance is simplified. An oil change every 500 miles or 30 days is a wise move in light of the fact that one oil is the only lubricant for all the critical wear areas in the engine.

The rubber-mounted dual carburetors are of the constant velocity type, and throttle response is excellent. A butterfly valve in the carburetor is actuated by the throttle cables. As this valve is opened by the twist grip, engine vacuum decreases and a diaphragm in the carburetor controls the opening of a second valve to allow passage of the fuel-air mixture in direct relation to the needs of the engine. Efficiency and ecomony are primary features, as fuel consumption is determined by vacuum, not the indiscriminate yank of the throttle cable by the rider. Air filtration is taken care of by two replaceable paper elements, which are easily reached by removal of the metal side covers.

The frame is a double loop, with a single top tube under the gas tank. The engine unit is snugly cradled between the mild steel tubing, and ample gusseting is placed at areas of stress around the fork head and the swinging arm pivot area. A stout tubular swinging arm contributes to the absense of undue flex and twist.

Vibration is minimal above an idle, suggesting that the frame is "well-tuned" to the engine. Stability on the road is evident at all speeds. Steering is precise, with a slight amount of understeer in the turns. The fork angle is suitable for a good road bike, and surface irregularities are overcome with only the slightest amount of handlebar wiggle.

Fork damping and spring rates are matched to the weight and type of road surfaces for which the machine is intended to be used. Yamaha is not trying to kid its prospective owners by calling the XS-650 a street-scrambler.

Appearance of the new Twin is excellent, with finish of the different components above average. Chrome steel fenders set off the black frame, while the candy paint gas tank is in keeping with the current trend towards attention-getting eye appeal. Individual tach and speedo heads, as well as the foot rests and handlebars, are rubber mounted. This eliminates the vibration tingle in the hands and feet that are so annoying after a few hours of riding. Control and seating position is just right, further assuring a comfortable ride.

One or two prods of the kick starter would bring the throaty Twin to life. Choking is necessary when the engine is cold and a two to three minute warm-up is required to allow the carburetors to respond correctly, another distinctly Japanese trait. The sound from the twin megaphone-styled mufflers is on the loud side, which will cause the public to notice the new machine quite readily. Unfortunately, the *gendarmerie* as well as our cranky senior citizens will be aware of its rumbling presence, and a trip to see the local judge might result, although Yamaha states they are fully approved.

The XS-650 felt quite at home on the winding roads of the Malibu mountains, with the brakes being the only components to show signs of fatigue. Yamaha has provided an air scoop on the front unit, and exhaust holes in the hub opposite the backing plate. Removal of the plate and plugs that cover these holes would facilitate brake cooling, and is advisable whenever heavy usage is contemplated.

In its introductory year, the XS-650 must be considered a *succes fou* (crazy success), having supplied all the ingredients required to please the big Twin fancier in an up-to-date, beautifully styled package. It looks good, rides good, stays clean and shows few of the faults one would expect in a first-year model.

As delivered, it performs on a par with its peers. The bonus: that new engine is a racing machine in disguise. For that reason, we fully expect that Yamaha's partial invasion of American "Class C" racing—limited previously to its rapid 250 and 350-cc road racers (and the 250 trackers)—will become complete in very short order.

YAMAHA R5 350

No Pseudo This Or Pseudo That, Yamaha's Updated Middleweight Does Its Proper Job At Modest Price.

YAMAHA HAS BROKEN away from the pseudo-scrambler school of styling for its street bikes, judging by the new R5 350.

No more high crossbar handlebars and bulky upswept exhaust systems. The R5 is sleek and most definitely a roadster, engineered for the rider who likes to straighten out a winding mountain road or cruise effortlessly down a freeway.

Yamaha hardly needs to fool the rider this way. If you want a scrambler with lights on, Yamaha has several in its line that really do the job.

The same effort that went into creation of the popular Enduro models has evidently been applied to the updating of the 350 roadster. It not only looks the part, but feels more comfortable and trustworthy in its natural habitat than its predecessors. The company has obviously benefited from its road racing experience with the successful 250-cc and 350-cc Class C road racers.

Overall appearance gives the machine a compact look over previous models. The impression is not unfounded; The new R5 is shorter, lower, slimmer and lighter than its forebearers. For one thing, the crankcase area is narrow, eliminating the spread eagle feeling associated with straddling the older Twins. The exhaust system is now one piece, eliminating the unsightly

joint between the head pipe and muffler. Also, with the narrower engine the pipes can be tucked in, allowing better ground clearance when banked over. The gasoline tank has been restyled along the lines of the classic early Triumph 500 Trophy. The lines flow well, blending into the new oil tank and side cover. This treatment is similar to the R5's big brother, the XS650. Finish of the paint, chrome fenders and other components is first rate, equal to anything on the market.

The aluminum cylinders, heads, and outer cases have a dull black finish. This serves to dissipate heat, and enhances the appearance of the engine. The outer edges of the fins and the raised ridges on the cases have been polished, giving the machine a classic mechanical look about it.

Finish on the alloy wheel hubs and lower fork legs is polished, and the fork shafts are chromed without covers. Slim-line road racing style front forks contribute to the appeal of the machine.

The individual tachometer and speedometer are rubber mounted, and have easy-to-read dials. Needle bounce and blur are non-existent, and a trip mileage indicator with reset knob is an added feature of the speedo. The ignition/lighting switch is mounted in an easy to reach spot just in front of the friction steering damper knob. Location of all controls is well thought out, with simplicity being the keynote.

This new 350 is basically similar to the first YR1, introduced in 1967 but with a multitude of improvements. The engine is an alternate firing vertical Twin, with 180 degree crankshaft configuration. Like all such designs, Yamaha's is inherently smooth running and free of vibration.

Internal refinements for the R5 include a bore/stroke change from a slightly oversquare 2.40 in. by 2.35 in., to an even more oversquare 2.51 in. by 2.12 in. This alteration results in a decrease of 1 cc in displacement, down from 348 to 347 cc. The apparent reasoning behind this is to present more surface area for wider ports, and reduce piston speed by shortening stroke.

Port openings are piston controlled, with the added 5th (or boost) port directing the fuel charge to the combustion area for better mid-range torque and cooling. Loads throughout the engine/transmission unit are carried by ball or needle bearings. Primary drive is by helical cut gears, sharing a common oil supply with the five speed transmission. The clutch is mounted on the transmission main shaft, and is encased in an aluminum housing.

The frame is mild steel tubing of duplex cradle design.

YAMAHA R5 350

SPECIFICATIONS

List price	$739 p.o.e.
Suspension, front	telescopic fork
Suspension, rear	swinging arm
Tire, front	3.00-18
Tire, rear	3.50-18
Brake, front, diameter x width, in.	7.2 x 1.18
Brake, rear, diameter x width, in.	7.2 x 1.18
Total brake swept area, sq. in.	52.8
Brake loading, lb./sq. in.	9.2
Engine, type	two-stroke Twin
Bore x stroke, in., mm	2.51 x 2.12, 64 x 54
Piston displacement, cu. in., cc	21.1, 347
Compression ratio	7.5
Carburetion	(2) Mikuni VMSC 28-mm
Ignition	battery and coil
Claimed bhp @ rpm	36 @ 7000
Oil system	oil injection
Oil capacity, pt.	4.2
Fuel capacity, U.S. gal.	3.2
Recommended fuel	premium
Starting system	kick, folding crank
Lighting system	12V, AC generator
Air filtration	paper element
Clutch	multi-disc, wet
Primary drive	gear
Final drive	3/8-in. x 5/8-in. chain
Gear ratios, overall:1	
5th	6.16
4th	7.38
3rd	9.12
2nd	12.15
1st	19.57
Wheelbase, in.	52.8
Seat height, in.	31.1
Seat width, in.	9.9
Handlebar width, in.	29.1
Footpeg height, in.	9.2
Ground clearance, in.	7.1
Curb weight (w/half-tank fuel), lb.	326
Weight bias, front/rear, percent	42/58
Test weight (fuel and rider), lb.	486

TEST CONDITIONS

Air temperature, degrees F	72
Humidity, percent	65
Barometric pressure, in. Hg.	29.80
Altitude above mean sea level, ft.	350
Wind velocity, mph	10-12
Strip alignment, relative wind:	

```
+-----------------------------------+
|              WIND                 |
| S  <----------------------->  F   |
+-----------------------------------+
```

PERFORMANCE

Top speed (actual @ 7960 rpm), mph	95.31
Computed top speed in gears (@ 8000 rpm), mph:	
5th	96
4th	80
3rd	65
2nd	55
1st	31
Mph/1000 rpm, top gear	11.98
Engine revolutions/mile, top gear	4996
Piston speed (@ 8000 rpm), ft./min.	2826
Fuel consumption, mpg	34
Speedometer error:	
50 mph indicated, actually	47.63
60 mph indicated, actually	57.85
70 mph indicated, actually	67.12
Braking distance:	
from 30 mph, ft.	36
from 60 mph, ft.	121
Acceleration, zero to:	
30 mph, sec.	2.5
40 mph, sec.	3.8
50 mph, sec.	4.9
60 mph, sec.	6.4
70 mph, sec.	9.0
80 mph, sec.	14.9
90 mph, sec.	24.4
Standing one-eighth mile, sec.	8.87
terminal speed, mph	69.60
Standing one-quarter mile, sec.	15.49
terminal speed, mph	81.08

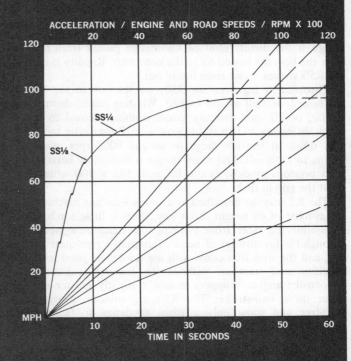

ACCELERATION / ENGINE AND ROAD SPEEDS / RPM X 100

Additional tubes and gussets have been added to reinforce the steering head and swinging-arm stress areas. This capable frame design is the direct result of knowledge gained from racing, with the benefits passed on to the consumer. Rigidity is one of the R5's virtues, as we soon found out.

Throwing a leg over the 350, we set out to see if she performed as well as she looked. Winding roads, downtown traffic, or 70 mph freeway grind, nothing seemed to make much difference to this stout two-stroke. Power is on tap from well down in the rev range to around 8000 rpm, where it begins to taper off. Mid range torque is noticeably better than with previous models, as the R5 pulls like a 500 when you twist the grip in fifth.

The R5 may be described as a quick handling machine. As it has most of its weight down low, there is little top hamper to inhibit the rider from pitching the machine aggressively through his favorite set of bends. Damping seems quite up to par, and the tires that come with the R5 deliver good tracking precision and traction. Without the braking qualities of a four-stroke engine, stoppers assume a slightly greater importance on a two-stroke. The R5's are smooth, progressive, grab-free and show only a slight tendency to fade under repeated use. Stopping distance from 60 mph (corrected) is exemplary.

We would like to see the wheelbase extended slightly to slow down the quick handling and put more weight on the front wheel. Shortness, coupled with the strong power range, had us leaning forward to keep the front end down during hard acceleration.

Day to day operation is another highlight of the R5's performance. Starting is a simple one-kick operation. Warm up time is less than a minute. Throttle response is quick and smooth thanks to minor jetting changes in the Mikuni carburetors. Shifting is effortless, and the ratios are well spaced to match the power band. All of the functions required to operate the machine are kept simple, eliminating quirks that distract from the pleasure of owning and riding a motorcycle.

During our test we did notice a bothersome noise that was present from the first ride: a rattling sound located inside the clutch/primary drive cover. It was most evident with the engine running and in neutral. As soon as the clutch lever was pulled in to disengage the clutch, the noise stopped. Upon checking with the Yamaha service department we were informed that this was probably caused by loose shock absorber springs located in the back of the clutch housing. When under tension they are rattle free, but given a little play, they emit a slight grumbling sound. Upon learning that no harm could come to the internals, we reluctantly put up with the noise and continued our test.

The R5 offers substance, as well as appearance. Within limits, it will do things most of the more expensive superbikes will do, at lesser cost but equal fun value. ◙

YAMAHA 200 CS3B

The "Almost 250." A Quick, Responsive Handler.

ENGINE DISPLACEMENT is a relative thing. Ideally, a powerplant should be large enough to do the job at hand, but no larger. It is a practical theory, but in reality, most bikes fall into certain classic displacement categories—125, 175, 250, 500, etc.

So what's the reasoning behind Yamaha's 200 CS3B, the "almost 250?" Well, it is the most recent update of another in-between displacement machine, the 180-cc CS1 which was introduced in 1967. The new version is 195cc. More displacement and more punch with minimal change in engine design, that's why the unusual size. And Yamaha's 200, which offers the added convenience of electric starting, is a very pleasant mount.

The engine runs well in the upper limits of its rpm range, and chassis components are more than up to the task of tackling curves on mountain roads at speeds. On level straight sections, the Yamaha 200 will run along at 8500 rpm in fifth cog (approximately 75 mph). Approach a right-hand curve, grab the brakes hard, downshift to fourth, and get back on the gas. At 7000 rpm, shift back into fifth and begin thinking about that next curve, a sharp left. Although handling is quite good, it is a bit quick due to a short, 49-in. wheelbase. Care, in fact, must be taken to avoid wheelies when accelerating hard in the first two gears. A 2.75-18 tire is fitted in front. The rear is a 3.00-18.

Forks are external spring, oil dampened units and the rear shock absorbers, featuring chrome springs, are three-way adjustable. A steering damper is also present that can be adjusted by rotating a large knurled knob located on top of the steering head.

The frame consists of a single toptube that curves downward just behind the engine. At this point, it is welded to plates that provide the rear engine mount and support the footpegs. A single front tube passes from the steering head down to the front of the engine. Tabs welded to this front tube form the forward engine mount.

The engine is used as a structural member and no tubing passes under it. The subframe, which supports the rear fender and seat, consists of two parallel tubes welded to the single toptube just at the rear of the gas tank. This subframe assembly is braced by an additional set of parallel tubes that pass from the rear engine mount to a point just in front of the rear shock absorbers. The rear shocks are mounted to tabs welded to this structure.

Back to those wheelies. Just because the 195-cc twin-cylinder, piston-port two-stroke is small, don't underestimate its

performance. Bore and stroke of each cylinder is 52 by 46mm. A claimed 22 bhp is produced at 7500 rpm and maximum torque is 15.7 lb.-ft. at 7000 rpm. Power is transmitted through a wet, multi-plate clutch to a five-speed, constant mesh transmission.

A four-main-bearing, 180-degree crankshaft is used. Needle bearings are fitted at the top and roller bearings at the bottom of each rod assembly. A center seal divides the two crankcase halves. Cylinders are five-ported. The fourth and fifth ports, which perform a booster function, are of the "tunnel" variety and are cast into the cylinders. Two 20-mm Mikuni carburetors deliver the fuel.

As with most small displacement Twins, the machine is a slightly reluctant starter from a dead stop without some clutch slipping, expecially with two aboard. Useable power begins at 3000 rpm and the unit pulls strongly from 5000 rpm right up to its 8200 rpm indicated redline. Because it has to be kept at a fairly high rpm most of the time, the noise level is higher than on some larger machines. You can feel engine vibration in the footpegs, but it is not too objectionable.

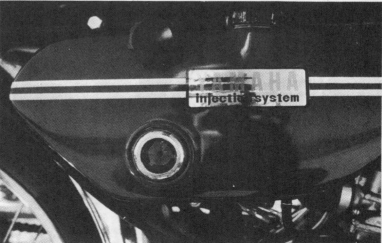

YAMAHA 200 CS3B

SPECIFICATIONS

List price	$619
Suspension, front	telescopic fork
Suspension, rear	swinging arm
Tire, front	2.75-18
Tire, rear	3.00-18
Brake, front, diameter x width, in.	7.08 x 1.18
Brake, rear, diameter x width, in.	5.90 x .98
Total brake swept area, sq. in.	44.40
Brake loading, lb./sq. in.	8.88
Engine, type	two-stroke Twin
Bore x stroke, in., mm	2.04 x 1.81, 52 x 46
Piston displacement, cu. in., cc	195
Compression ratio	7.1:1
Claimed bhp @ rpm	22 @ 7500
Claimed torque @ rpm, lb.-ft.	15.7 @ 7000
Carburetion	(2) 20-mm Mikuni
Ignition	battery and coil
Oil system	oil injection
Oil capacity, pt.	4.0
Fuel capacity, U.S. gal.	2.4
Recommended fuel	regular
Starting system	electric, kick
Lighting system	12-V alternator
Air filtration	dry paper
Clutch	multi-plate, wet
Primary drive	helical gear
Final drive	chain
Gear ratios, overall: 1	
5th	7.96
4th	9.90
3rd	13.46
2nd	17.77
1st	26.84
Wheelbase, in.	49
Seat height, in.	30.5
Seat width, in.	10.5
Handlebar width, in.	27.5
Footpeg height, in.	10.0
Ground clearance, in.	6.5 (at stand)
Curb weight (w/half-tank fuel), lb.	264
Weight bias, front/rear, percent	44/56
Test weight (fuel and rider), lb.	394

TEST CONDITIONS

Air temperature, degrees F	68
Humidity, percent	45
Barometric pressure, in. hg.	30.31
Altitude above mean sea level, ft.	50
Wind velocity, mph	3-6
Strip alignment, relative wind:	

```
                    WIND
                           /
 S  >──────────────────────────>  F
                         /
                        ↙
```

PERFORMANCE

Top speed (actual @ 8680 rpm), mph	76.33
Computed top speed in gears (@ 8200 rpm), mph:	
5th	72
4th	58
3rd	43
2nd	32
1st	21
Mph/1000 rpm, top gear	8.8
Engine revolutions/mile, top gear	6840
Piston speed (@ 8200 rpm), ft./min.	2470
Lb./hp (test wt.)	17.9
Speedometer error:	
50 mph indicated, actually	46.7
60 mph indicated, actually	56.6
70 mph indicated, actually	66.2
Braking distance:	
from 30 mph, ft.	34.1
from 60 mph, ft.	142.0
Acceleration, zero to:	
30 mph, sec.	4.2
40 mph, sec.	5.9
50 mph, sec.	7.7
60 mph, sec.	10.0
70 mph, sec.	14.7
Standing one-eighth mile, sec.	10.34
terminal speed, mph	61.30
Standing one-quarter mile, sec.	17.05
terminal speed, mph	72.99

ACCELERATION / ENGINE AND ROAD SPEEDS / RPM X 100

Brakes are smooth and do not grab. Pedal and lever pressure is light. Straight-line stops are the rule, and little fade is encountered after repeated abuse.

As on other Yamahas, Autolube is featured. Gas/oil mixing is automatic. All the rider need do is keep the separate oil tank full. At idle, the gas/oil ratio is approximately 120-150:1. As the throttle is opened and rpm increases, more oil is added. At full throttle, depending on the rpm, the gas/oil ratio will change to approximately 16:1. Less chance of fouling spark plugs and less exhaust smoke are two of the more obvious advantages.

The oil tank is located on the right side of the machine. Its filler cap is partially covered by the seat, but unlike other Yamahas, the tank itself, instead of the seat, is hinged to provide access. Oil capacity is 2.0 quarts. A metal cover, on the opposite side of the Yamaha 200, conceals the toolbox, 12V battery, and a cylindrical air cleaner canister. Two dry paper air filter elements are fitted, one in each end of the canister.

Both a speedometer and a tachometer are provided. They are attractive, easily read, and rubber mounted. Instrument lights, however, are too bright and are annoying when the machine is ridden at night. The speedometer scale goes to 100 mph, but does not feature a resettable trip odometer. The tachometer is sluggish, especially when successive rapid shifts are executed near redline in the lower gears. The indicator lights include a green neutral indicator light on the far left, an

amber turn signal indicator light in the center, and a red generator light at the far right.

The ignition switch, conveniently located between the instruments, is also rubber mounted. A fork lock, located between the fork legs just under the headlight, is present. However, no protective cover is provided to keep out dirt.

Turn signals are standard equipment, and their controls are located in the left handgrip housing, as are switches for the horn and high/low, on/off lighting switches.

The handlebar/seat/footpeg relationship is excellent for riding around town, but slightly lower bars would improve rider comfort at freeway speeds. Handlebar width is narrower than that on the average road machine designed for the American market, but this is advantageous as it helps to keep the arms out of the air stream. Air currents flailing against widely spread arms can cause the front end of the bike to jiggle at high speeds.

Overall finish and appearance is quite good. The 2.4-gal. gas tank, side panels and headlight are painted purple. White pinstriping accents the tank and side panels. Fenders are chrome plated, fork legs are highly polished, and the deeply padded seat is black.

With an operating range of slightly over 100 miles, and because it is turning a little over 7000 rpm at freeway speeds, the Yamaha 200 is not an ideal high speed tourer. But then it wasn't intended to be. It's quick, responsive, and fills both a price ($619) and a displacement gap. ◙

YAMAHA XS-2
A Stud Bike With A Starter,
And One Helluva Stopper!

YAMAHA, BUILDERS OF some of the fastest two-cycle motorcycles in the world, surprised the American motorcycling public late in 1969 with the introduction of the XS-1, a large-capacity four-stroke laid out in the "English tradition" with two vertical cylinders and an alternately firing, 360-degree crankshaft.

Knowing the appeal that the big British vertical Twin has to the American rider, the people at Yamaha set about improving both design and execution, while retaining the power, handling characteristics, and styling of this type of motorcycle.

The engine and transmission are in one unit, but the crankcase is split horizontally instead of vertically, which allows an assembly with fewer sections, and fewer places to leak oil. This design simplifies the use of a four-main-bearing crankshaft which, in the case of the XS-2, is a pressed-together, or "built-up," unit employing four flywheels. Three roller bearings and one ball bearing (next to the clutch on the right-hand side) support the crankshaft assembly, and the connecting rods ride on roller bearings instead of the more common plain bearings. Although there are four separate flywheels, the net effect is less than most machines with a single flywheel; the XS-2 is quite "buzzy" and quick to respond to small changes in throttle opening.

A chain-drive sprocket in the center of the crankshaft is used to drive the overhead camshaft, and new for this year are the teeth on one flywheel to permit the engagement of the electric Bendix-type starter's gears. The starter unit itself nestles in a cavity below the transmission (which reduces the engine/transmission oil capacity from 3 qt. to 2.5 qt.) and is triggered by a compression release-type handle below the throttle on the right handlebar. Squeezing this lever raises the left cylinder's exhaust valve to ease the starter's work, and simultaneously triggers a micro-switch which starts the current flowing. A safety device is designed into the circuit to prevent starter actuation while the engine is running, and to disengage the starter unit once the engine fires up.

Power from the crankshaft is transmitted to the clutch by straight-cut gears, which are surprisingly quiet. Five metal and six friction plates are used to provide one of the best oil bath clutches we've encountered. Even though the clutch lever is now closer to the handlebar, with a subsequent reduction in the lever travel possible, the clutch never got so hot while sitting at a stoplight with the bike in gear that we couldn't find neutral easily.

Many full-throttle standing start quarter-mile acceleration runs at Lions Drag Strip failed to make it protest, but the lever had to be adjusted slightly one time during the runs. The one part of the clutch mechanism we didn't like was the method of cushioning the hub from the engine's power impulses. Six coil springs are set into the back of the driven gear assembly (clutch hub) which tend to "wind up" as the clutch is being released from a standstill. Then, just before the clutch fully engages, the springs "unwind," a clunk is heard, and the machine creeps forward slightly before the drive is taken up. The cushioning device is needed, as there is no such device incorporated into the rear wheel, but the substitution of neoprene-type rubber blocks for the springs in the design would cure this annoying problem.

The transmission itself, with the exception of a slightly lower first gear, remains unchanged from earlier models. A circular shifting drum with three girdling shifter forks move the all-indirect ratio gears back and forth on the layshaft and mainshaft, both of which are supported by needle bearings on one end and a ball bearing on the other end. Shifting is all but effortless, but there was a hint of vagueness at times when the engine was hot. The closeness of the gear ratios makes the bike seem more like a road racer than a roadster, and the engine's smooth, broad power band makes the five speeds seem almost superfluous.

Continuing upward, the three-ring (two compression and one oil control ring) pistons run on bushings at the top of the connecting rods, as opposed to the needle bearings found in earlier models. A cast iron sleeve is located in the finned aluminum cylinder casting on either side of a tunnel for the camshaft chain. At the rear is the cam chain tensioner wheel and adjustment screw, and a long, rubber-faced chain damper assembly is placed in the front of the cylinder casting. A total of eight hold-down studs secure the cylinder and head to the crankcase.

The cylinder head is a smooth aluminum alloy casting with moderately shallow combustion chambers, straight-in inlet ports and slightly splayed exhaust ports to promote better cylinder head cooling. Double coil valve springs close the valves, and valve guide seals are provided to prevent oil from being used excessively. The intake balance tube between the inlet ports has disappeared.

The hollow camshaft is supported by two ball bearings on each side, and its left and right ends are used to drive the ignition contact points and the spark advance mechanism. A detachable rocker box houses four separate rocker shafts, each with a finger-type cam follower. Valve clearance adjustment is accomplished through three triangular and one roughly square (at the left exhaust valve position) leak-proof covers.

Oil for the XS-2's internals is circulated by a trochoidal pump which features four inner vanes and five outer vanes. Both rotors turn together, but rotate at different speeds and create a gap between themselves which is filled with oil. Hence, there is an almost smooth flow of lubricant to the crankshaft main and connecting rod bearings, transmission mainshaft, clutch bearing and shifting mechanism. Oil for the rocker arms and valve gear is delivered through a pipe at the front of the cylinder. "Splash" lubrication is used to lubricate the crankshaft, small end bearings, pistons and cylinder walls, and the primary drive gears. A bypass valve redirects oil around the oil filter and back into the oil reservoir if the pressure becomes too great.

Mikuni "constant velocity" carburetors, manufactured under license from Solex, provide outstanding throttle response and amazing fuel economy, as well as smooth idling. A butterfly valve located downstream of the needle controls the amount of air coming into the front (intake end) of the carburetor. A rubber diaphragm is connected to the top of the slide (piston valve) which divides the top part of the carburetor into a vacuum chamber. An air bleed hole which leads to the underside of the diaphragm admits air at atmospheric pressure to that area, and a hole in the bottom of the slide leads to the top of the vacuum chamber. As the butterfly is opened a vacuum is generated beneath the slide and it rises according to the opening of the butterfly valve. Hence, it is impossible to flood the engine by using the throttle too vigorously, as the slide will rise no higher to admit more fuel/air mixture than the engine can use.

Electrical chores are handled admirably by a crankshaft-mounted alternator whose a.c. current is rectified to d.c. by a three-phase, full-wave rectifier. The flow to the battery, as well as a trickle to excite the rotor windings, to promote current production, is controlled by a voltage regulator. A 14-15V d.c. current is kept flowing into the new, larger 12V-12AH battery, which is plenty large enough to drive the electric starter, the main lighting system and the turn signals. Electrical components, of course, are first rate.

Bottom view of upper crankcase with crankshaft assembly in place. Note starter gear teeth on the left flywheel.

Starter motor shown removed for clarity. Small-sized unit is capable of tremendous torque.

Mikuni CV carburetor and air cleaner assembly. Dry paper elements effectively filter air, keep intake noise to a minimum.

Basically unchanged is the double loop, cradle-type frame with a single large toptube running under the gas tank. Ample support is provided for the engine, which is rigidly mounted in the frame, and liberal gusseting around the steering head and swinging arm pivot offer a true tracking machine. Our first test of the 650-cc Yamaha revealed what felt like a hinge right under the seat when the machine was banked over hard in a corner. However, better rear suspension units and slightly stiffer front suspension with redesigned damping has all but cured this problem. Front fork action is almost too soft for best control at high speeds over rough surfaces, but slightly heavier oil would help the "wallowing" at the expense of a slightly stiffer ride. The footpegs are set rather low to the ground, and can be grounded without too much trouble when negotiating fast sweepers, but the average rider should have no problems. With so much of the engine's weight up high, there

YAMAHA XS-2

SPECIFICATIONS

List price	$1295 p.o.e. West Coast
Suspension, front	telescopic fork
Suspension, rear	swinging arm
Tire, front	3.25-19
Tire, rear	4.00-18
Brake, front, diameter x width, in.	(2) 11.68 x 1.85
Brake, rear, diameter x width, in.	7.1 x 1.1
Total brake swept area, sq. in.	86.8
Brake loading, lb./sq. in.	5.24
Engine, type	sohc vertical Twin
Bore x stroke, in., mm	2.95 x 2.91, 75 x 74
Piston displacement, cu. in., cc	39.8, 653
Compression ratio	8.7:1
Claimed bhp @ rpm	53 @ 7000
Claimed torque @ rpm, lb.-ft.	40.1 @ 6000
Carburetion	(2) Mikuni CV 30mm
Ignition	coil and battery
Oil system	wet sump, vane-type pump
Oil capacity, pt.	5.0
Fuel capacity, U.S. gal.	3.3
Recommended fuel	premium
Starting system	electric; kick, folding crank
Lighting system	12-V alternator
Air filtration	dry paper
Clutch	multi-disc, wet
Primary drive	gear
Final drive	single-row chain
Gear ratios, overall:1	
5th	5.10
4th	5.85
3rd	6.94
2nd	8.48
1st	13.16
Wheelbase, in.	56.0
Seat height, in.	32.0
Seat width, in.	11.5
Handlebar width, in.	31.0
Footpeg height, in.	10.0
Ground clearance, in.	6.0
Curb weight (w/half-tank fuel), lb.	455
Weight bias, front/rear, percent	45/55
Test weight (fuel and rider), lb.	585
Mileage at completion of test	2178

TEST CONDITIONS

Air temperature, degrees F	84
Humidity, percent	62
Barometric pressure, in. hg.	31.70
Altitude above mean sea level, ft.	50
Wind velocity, mph	4-8
Strip alignment, relative wind:	

WIND
S ——————► F

PERFORMANCE

Top speed (actual @ 7130 rpm), mph	107.1
Computed top speed in gears (@ 7500 rpm), mph	
5th	11.
4th	9
3rd	8
2nd	6
1st	4
Mph/1000 rpm, top gear	15.
Engine revolutions/mile, top gear	398
Piston speed (@ 7500 rpm), ft./min.	363
Lb./hp (test wt.)	10.
Fuel consumption, mpg	5
Speedometer error:	
50 mph indicated, actually	44.
60 mph indicated, actually	53.
70 mph indicated, actually	63.
Braking distance:	
from 30 mph, ft.	34.
from 60 mph, ft.	129.
Acceleration, zero to:	
30 mph, sec.	2.9
40 mph, sec.	3.9
50 mph, sec.	4.8
60 mph, sec.	5.6
70 mph, sec.	7.4
80 mph, sec.	9.2
90 mph, sec.	13.6
100 mph, sec.	21.9
Standing one-eighth mile, sec.	9.04
terminal speed, mph	79.30
Standing one-quarter mile, sec.	14.07
terminal speed, mph	92.9

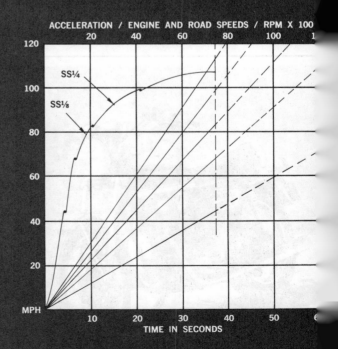

ACCELERATION / ENGINE AND ROAD SPEEDS / RPM X 100

SS¼

SS⅛

TIME IN SECONDS

YAMAHA XS-2

is still a feeling of top-heaviness at crawling speed, but this feeling disappears as you accelerate.

A friction-type steering damper is useful when traveling at high speeds, as the front end has a slight tendency to "search" and sets up a slight "wallow" at turnpike speeds. If the damper is left screwed down while riding in town, the machine feels very clumsy. Loosening the damper only a little, however, cures this sensation, and the XS-2 feels almost as nimble as a good 350. A wide, comfortable dual seat used in conjunction with the rather low-mounted footpegs makes long touring very comfortable. Our only exception to the control group is the handlebars, which look as though they came off Keith Mashburn's flat tracker! They're a bit too far swept back for comfort in the wrist area when seated on the front half of the

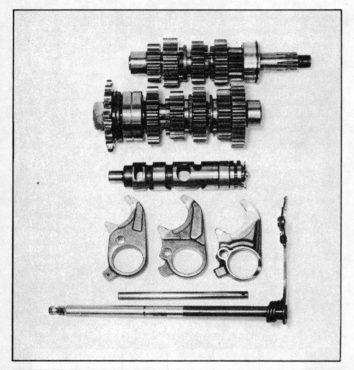

seat. Scoot back on the seat and they feel neat, but too far and you'll have your passenger sitting on the fender! However, they can't be all bad, as one of our staff riders, whose physique resembles that of a well-fed spider, thought they were just dandy.

The addition of the powerful disc brake to the front wheel is one of the most outstanding improvements made for 1972. The caliper unit is bolted directly to the right-hand fork leg and resists wheel cocking when the brake is applied hard. Only two fingers are necessary to lock the front wheel under any conditions, so caution is the word at first. The brake lever operates the master cylinder directly and features an adjustment screw and lock nut, allowing the rider to vary the point where the brake begins to engage. This is extremely nice for riders with short fingers or small hands. As is common practice with motorcycle disc brakes, the disc is fabricated out of a stainless steel alloy instead of cast iron. An iron disc is more effective and somewhat quieter in operation than a stainless compound, but iron rusts rapidly and spoils the appearance of the motorcycle. The Yamaha's front brake squeals loudly when slowing from moderate speeds, so we hope that quieter brake pads are in the offing. Disc brakes are more expensive than drum brakes, but with so many powerful machines on the road today with less than excellent stopping ability, we expect to see discs on more machines as the year progresses.

The rear brake, which does only a moderate amount of the stopping chore, is a conventional single-leading shoe affair that performs very well and is slow to heat up and fade. No adjustment of the rear brake was necessary during the test, and of course the front brake is self-adjusting.

A few of our other minor complaints against the first XS-1 have been rectified by Yamaha. One of the most vehement of these concerned the vibration occurring throughout the engine's rpm range over idle speed. Changes made to the crankshaft's balance factor have helped out enormously. Rubber-mounted handlebars and footpegs have been employed since the first models to help stifle the vibration, and now the combination really works. Practically no vibration gets past the handlebars, and only a tingle is felt in the footpegs at highway speeds.

Another of our complaints was the noise made by the megaphone-type mufflers. It was not only loud, but also had a peculiar "nasal" quality about it which was particularly obnoxious to several of our staff members. Happily, Yamaha has made several changes in the baffling arrangement, and the result is an authoritative, yet pleasant, sound. There is almost no mechanical noise from the engine and, as in the past, the unit is almost free from oil leaks. Changes to washers and seal design have made the XS-2 even more oil tight than before.

Instrumentation is very good, but the speedometer is quite optimistic. A neutral indicator light and turn signal indicator are located in the tachometer face, and the high beam indicator is a red light in the top of the headlight. All thumb-operated controls are well shaped, within easy reach of the handle grips, and the ignition switch is ensconced between the speedometer and tachometer, obviating the need to fumble around under the gas tank.

Power delivery is among the smoothest we've sampled on a machine of this engine configuration. Power comes on strong as low as 2000 rpm and continues in a smooth surge well past the 7500-rpm red-line. Several of the ohc Yamahas being used for racing are being spun in excess of 9000 rpm!

The XS-2 is undoubtedly the best buy in a machine of its type. The sum total of its parts makes it a sporting machine without equal, a stud with a starter, promising great times on the boulevards with few maintenance hassles. ◙

■ How much performance and styling do you get in a roadster the size of a small trailbike? Are they practical or just toys?

Actually, if you are forced to hassle cross-town traffic daily, or if riding flat-out on twisty roads turns you on, lightweights like Yamaha's 100- or 200cc street Twins are not a bad way to go.

There are several reasons for this, the first of which is low initial cost. Monetary savings don't stop there, either. Because they are small, gas mileage is outstanding. Maintenance is simple, which should keep labor charges low, and if anything major breaks, parts are cheap.

Economics are important, but no one is going to buy a drab scooter that can't keep up with traffic. That's precisely why Yamaha doesn't build any bikes in that category. Both the 100 and 200 are everything the superlative 250 is; only on a smaller, less expensive scale.

Take styling. Chromed fenders and exhausts accent tastefully pinstriped gas tanks and side panels on both machines. Instrumentation is complete with a tachometer and speedometer. There are also turn signals, and each motorcycle is fitted with passenger pegs and a comfortable dual seat.

Cycle World Road Test

Their real selling point, though, is the very thing that people tend to be most skeptical about regarding small bikes. Performance. The 200 is a jet. Period. It will pull wheelies off the line, can pass cars at will on mountain roads, and will survive mile after mile of freeway with the engine spinning at 7000 rpm or so. Several older 250s will not be able to keep pace, especially where handling enters into it.

Handling is rather quick, but nowhere near the point of being dangerous. Steering is precise and there is ample ground clearance to allow the 200 to be banked way over for turns. Nothing scrapes and the suspension never falters with a 160 lb.

YAMAHA 200 CS5 AND 100 LS2

Meet The Little Twins:
If You Have To Start Small,
There Are Few Better Ways To Do So

YAMAHA

rider aboard. Heavier loads, though, will cause the new internal-spring front legs to bottom, especially when braking on rough roads.

Brakes are more than adequate for a 200cc machine. The front unit is double-leading shoe. It has good feel and offers the added benefit of light hand lever pressure. The rear brake is a conventional single-shoe drum with rod linkage.

Riding the 200 is fun, but in some ways the 100 is more enjoyable. True, it isn't legal on freeways which makes the 200 more versatile, but the 100 is easier to live with in town. It's so nimble that traffic seems less bothersome. The 100 is quite competitive in stoplight grand prixs, too, as long as the revs are kept up and the five-speed gearbox is used to best advantage. We're not saying that you can blow off the big iron, but quite a few compacts will fall behind until 40 mph or so.

The 100 is more than a cross-town commuter. Truck it to your favorite stretch of winding country road (the tighter the

turns the better) and you will be entertained for hours. A top speed of 60 mph is attainable with the rider sitting up and this can be improved on slight downhills or by tucking in close to the gas tank. Just how much improvement depends on the conditions (wind direction, etc.), but 70 mph is possible if a 9000 rpm tach reading doesn't scare you off.

Because of its light weight, small size and good traction, cornering ability really exceeds the power available. Technique, therefore, is simple. Hold the throttle wide open in the highest gear the engine will pull, and dive into anything short of a hairpin. Don't be fooled, though. The little Twin will wail along at speeds often exceeding legality and common sense.

Unfortunately, suspension is not on the same level as the bigger 200. Especially the rear shocks. Damping is non-existent, resulting in a near-constant, slow-motion bouncing action that is more annoying than anything else. The front forks are

200 CS5

SPECIFICATIONS

List price	$649
Suspension, front	telescopic fork
Suspension, rear	swinging arm
Tire, front	2.75-18
Tire, rear	3.00-18
Engine, type	two-stroke Twin
Bore x stroke, in., mm	2.05 x 1.81, 52 x 46
Piston displacement, cu. in., cc	11.9, 195
Compression ratio	7.1:1
Claimed bhp @ rpm	22 @ 7500
Claimed torque @ rpm, lb.-ft.	15.7 @ 7000
Piston speed (@ rpm), ft./min.	2262 @ 7500
Carburetion	(2) Mikuni VM 20 SC
Ignition	battery and coil
Oil system	oil injection
Oil capacity, pt.	4.0
Fuel capacity, U.S. gal.	2.4
Recommended fuel	premium
Starting system	electric; kick, folding crank
Air filtration	dry paper
Clutch	multi-disc, wet
Primary drive	gear
Final drive	single-row chain
Gear ratios, overall:1	
5th	7.75
4th	9.65
3rd	13.11
2nd	17.30
1st	26.15

DIMENSIONS

Wheelbase, in.	49
Seat height, in.	30.0
Seat width, in.	9.5
Handlebar width, in.	29.5
Footpeg height, in.	10.5
Ground clearance, in.	8.0
Curb weight (w/half-tank fuel), lb.	281
Weight bias, front/rear, percent	44.5/55.5

PERFORMANCE

Standing quarter-mile, sec.	17.24
Terminal speed, mph	67.71

100 LS2

SPECIFICATIONS

List price	$453
Suspension, front	telescopic fork
Suspension, rear	swinging arm
Tire, front	2.50-18
Tire, rear	2.50-18
Engine, type	two-stroke Twin
Bore x stroke, in., mm	1.49 x 1.69, 38 x 43
Piston displacement, cu. in., cc	5.91, 97
Compression ratio	7.0:1
Claimed bhp @ rpm	10.5 @ 8000
Claimed torque @ rpm, lb.-ft.	6.95 @ 7500
Piston speed (@ rpm), ft./min.	2258 @ 8000
Carburetion	(2) Mikuni VM 17 SC
Ignition	battery and coil
Oil system	oil injection
Oil capacity, pt.	3.0
Fuel capacity, U.S. gal.	2.0
Recommended fuel	premium
Starting system	kick, folding crank
Air filtration	dry paper
Clutch	multi-disc, wet
Primary drive	gear
Final drive	single-row chain
Gear ratios, overall:1	
5th	9.81
4th	12.21
3rd	15.19
2nd	21.18
1st	37.17

DIMENSIONS

Wheelbase, in.	47.5
Seat height, in.	29.5
Seat width, in.	9.0
Handlebar width, in.	27.0
Footpeg height, in.	10.25
Ground clearance, in.	8.0
Curb weight (w/half-tank fuel), lb.	229
Weight bias, front/rear, percent	44.5/55.5

PERFORMANCE

Standing quarter-mile, sec.	20.33
Terminal speed, mph	59.24

adequate in both damping and travel; but like the rear units, they could stand some improvement.

Braking is the only other area in which the 100 falls a little short. Because of its lighter weight and lower power output, Yamaha has fitted single-leading shoe brakes at both ends. The rear brake is fine, but the front has a spongy feel, requires considerable lever pressure in a panic stop, and will fade with repeated abuse.

Still, it must be rated along with the larger 200 as a better than average handler. This is due to a strong, although quite unusual, frame design that is similar on both bikes. It's unusual because the engine is used as a structural member. A single toptube (with additional bracing on the 200) curves downward behind the engine where it connects to a box-like structure that forms the rear engine mount. When the front downtube is bolted to the engine, the structure becomes quite rigid. The swinging arm assembly pivots from the same structure that forms the rear engine mount. A subframe supporting the rear fender and seat completes the package.

The engines are more conventional. Both are two-stroke, parallel Twins with five-ported cylinders, twin carburetors, and autolube oil-injection. Gear primary drives deliver 22 and 10.5 bhp respectively from 180-degree crankshafts to wet, multi-disc clutches and five-speed transmissions.

Starting is easy in both cases. The 100 has a primary kick starter which seldom requires more than two prods. The 200 with its electric starter fires instantly at the touch of a button. A kickstarter is fitted for emergencies but it will not be needed as long as the 12-volt battery is properly maintained.

Now, back to the question. Do small bikes like these offer enough performance to be practical? The answer is an unqualified yes if you're not a freeway freak or long distance touring type. And, Yamaha's small displacement Twins have that one additional advantage—economical operation. ⬛

YAMAHA'S COUNTERBALANCED, DISC-BRAKED, DOUBLE OVERHEAD CAM, TWO-CYLINDER AND (AHA!) SOMEWHAT SELF-DIAGNOSTIC MOTORCYCLE

RIDING AN INNOVATIVE PROTOTYPE

BY DAN HUNT

IT MAY SEEM curious that Yamaha is spending money developing yet another four-stroke Twin, when the whole world is going to multis.

On the other hand, Yamaha may be smart and we don't know it. After all, the big Twin, by which I mean any vertical Twin of 650 to 750cc displacement, is a popular size and shape of bike. Not too large for a hop up the block. Not so small that it can't smoke off anything on up to about a small-block Corvette, costing four times as much money.

With the new TX750, Yamaha seems to have rethought the whole idea of what the Big Twin is supposed to be. Fiddling around with public preconceptions must make that company more than a little nervous.

A ride on the bike tells you that Yamaha is only incidentally pitting this Twin against other Twins—like Bonnevilles, Commandos, Lightnings and dohc 450s. The TX750's real goal is a flanking assault on the expensive segment of the multi-cylinder which, of course, includes Honda's 500 and 750 Fours, Kawasaki's 750 Three, the British Triples, and Suzuki's big waterpumper.

The idea of anyone competing against the big multis with a Twin may seem preposterous. Unless you can make the Twin as good as or almost as good as the multis and offer it for less

IS THIS THE BIRTH OF COMPUTERIZED SERVICING?

WOULD YOU BE more likely to buy a motorcycle if it could tell you in a few seconds what it was that ailed it? Yamaha is betting that you will, and has made the opening move with a diagnostic panel on its prototype TX750. If the consumer and the rest of the industry responds positively, a new era will be upon us.

"Diagnostics" is not entirely new. Volkswagen owners are getting acquainted with a system which yields an instantaneous reading of the several points in the automobile. This system is basically oriented to the service technician, who plugs a lead from an expensive computer console into a multi-pronged receptacle in the automobile engine compartment.

After going through a prescribed testing routine, the technician has secured readouts for 15 or 16 conditions—i.e., battery voltage under various loads, operation of all lights, engine compression, condition of the ignition system, alternator charging, and front end alignment.

While VW's system only probes the surface of the automobile's condition, the hook-up between car and computer provides for about 150 different pieces of information. If

money. For the multi class, what is good is "smooth." And you know that typical vertical Twins are inherently not smooth. They vibrate, either because of primary imbalance created as the pistons churn up-and-down in unison, or because of eccentric vibration patterns created by 180-degree crankshaft layouts.

Many ways have been contrived to civilize the Twin. BMW succeeded in fair fashion by opposing cylinders horizontally and tolerating a small amount of rocking couple and throttle-induced torque reaction. Harley-Davidson went to a 45-degree V pattern and didn't succeed at all. Moto Guzzi and Ducati have chosen the 90-degree V, which is better but by no means perfect, due to a strong horizontal force vector.

Now it appears that Yamaha has made the whole thing academic by using the vertical Twin configuration with a new twist. Counterbalancing.

In principle, it's a simple measure. Yamaha uses chain-driven internal bobweights which counter the primary imbalances created by the vertical Twin arrangement. The bobweights, being off-center, swing in opposition to the pistons, etc.

The result is smoothness beyond belief. Shut your eyes and you are on a Four. It couldn't be a Twin. The engine doesn't lope or rock the bike at idle. The handlebars don't feel like they're carrying live house current when you're pushing along at 5000 rpm. The image in the rear view mirror doesn't fragment into myriad circular patterns when you crank the TX up to the 7000 rpm redline when running through the gears.

To shatter the bubbles a bit, it should be noted that Yamaha doesn't come by that smoothness without paying for it. Bobweights are exactly what they say they are—weights.>

Yamaha's method of incorporating exhaust crosstube into a bolt-on "manifold" eliminates possible cracking, blueing of joints. Clever idea.

these possible readouts are intelligently exploited, the advantages in terms of time saved and increased objectivity and accuracy of diagnosis are great. The diagnostician hands you the readout sheet and it's up to you *what* points you fix and *where* you'll have it fixed.

Yamaha's system is hardly a system at this stage. It is a promise. A challenge to the motorcycle industry. An invitation to a dialogue of oneupmanship.

As such, it is a consumer-oriented system in its present form. Out there, below the speedometer, you may read three gauges that tell you a) your oil pressure, b) rear brake lining condition and c) taillight operation.

Oil pressure is no big deal, but in the context of the other two lights, is most definitely a diagnostic light, rather than one that indicates transient condition. The taillight indicator is not a strikingly difficult one to devise—you merely wire the indicator lamp in series with the tail lamp—and you can take it or leave it (you'll probably leave it if you find looking over your shoulder a less costly alternative).

The clincher though is the brake lining indicator light which comes on when the lining gets low. Here, for the first time in motorcycling history, the rider is given instant and specific warning of the impending failure of an important component *before* the failure occurs.

It is common knowledge that a worn rear brake lining is not dangerous (in that the front brake does most of the work), and so you may wonder why Yamaha goes to the trouble. In one way, it is the typical sales gimmick. Another blinking gew-gaw to woo a fickle buying public. But in the long-term view of

Will motorcycle instrumentation evolve from a simple cluster of lights...

...To a computerized system of diagnostics like this?

INNOVATIVE PROTOTYPE

The TX's curb weight is 520 lb., which is even more than the Honda 750 Four (500 lb.) and only a few pounds less than the Suzuki Watercooled 750 (524 lb.).

The extra weight will tend to inhibit the performance of the TX750, which doesn't have as impressive a power-to-weight ratio as its predecessor, the SX-2. To compensate for this, Yamaha is playing with lower gearing than normal. Taking 7000 rpm as the upper limit, the particular machine we rode was geared for about 101 mph in 5th.

On the usual Twin, this high revving could create a great deal of discomfort at highway speeds, yet the counterbalanced Yamaha can get by quite nicely because the comfort factor isn't dependent on the rpm at which the engine is turning. The overall ratios for public consumption have yet to be chosen, so keep in mind that the ones published in our data panel are only tentative and may be different on the showroom models.

Yamaha hopes to cash in with this smooth, heavy motorcycle by underselling the big multis, and offering a less bothersome package. As the bike is a Twin, it is somewhat easier to maintain than a Three or a Four. The TX750 has only two carburetors to balance, two spark plugs, two pistons and two sets of rings, fewer bearing surfaces, etc. The added complexity of the double overhead camshaft or the bobweight system will be a minor factor in respect to maintenance.

While Yamaha would have preferred to drive the double bobweights by gear, to avoid the adjustment schedule of chain drive, they found the gears too noisy in earlier prototypes. Switching to chain drive silenced the machine, from which emanates now the sporting sounds of whirring and clicking camshafts, noticeable but pleasant.

Yamaha's disc-brake system features double-acting caliper arrangement and an additional disc may be easily fitted on the other fork.

COMPUTERIZED SERVICING?

things, that little gimmick is also a market test. To get public reaction you have to put it out on the handlebars where the public can see it.

Ironically, if the brake lining light is successful, in a few years it will disappear into a black box under the seat with several other component status readout junctions. Why? Even though it would be possible to build a 20-item instrument panel on the motorcycle, it would be costly and of dubious benefit to the rider.

The reasons are clear. By reserving the diagnostic readout for the technician's eyes alone, you keep the motorcycle relatively simple. You also protect the motorcycle from the individual who is overly anxious to make conclusions based upon a complex combination of instrument readouts. And you lower manufacturing cost; complex panels, besides being expensive in themselves, also have extra power and space requirements. By instead offering a junction box which may be joined with an external diagnostic console, you externalize the extra power supply and component needs. The console provides its own power for the tests to be made.

It is amazing how much information may be culled from a mechanical entity by relatively simple means. The Yamaha

brake lining light, for example, consists of a wire running to a contact fixed near the brake shoe actuating cam. When the lining wears down, the cam turns far enough to make electrical contact. The motorcycle frame is used as electrical ground so only one wire is needed to reach the sensor.

The brake lining readout is what may be termed a "yes or no" situation. Yes, the lining is good. No, the lining is not good. Any situation like this offers an extremely simple situation for computer analysis.

If and when Yamaha or other manufacturers get to the external console stage, however, they will want to take more complex measurements. For example, cylinder pressure without the engine firing is one example of a measurement that defies simple "good" or "not good" diagnosis. It is rather an acceptable *range* of cylinder pressure which must be subjectively interpreted before you can flatly declare that the patient needs a valve job.

If you hand test a cylinder, you are in effect taking an analog, or progressively quantitative, reading which is not diagnostic in itself. You are functioning as part of the instrument to make the diagnosis. Your mind is programmed by the shop manual. It tells you that the reading will be 125 to 150 psi. Below 125 psi, something's really wrong. Readout: valve job.

If, instead, you mechanize this whole process, you must invent a diagnostic instrument which works essentially as a simple computer. The sensor gives a continuous reading along the scale from 125 to 150 psi. An electronic device known as a

YAMAHA TX750

SPECIFICATIONS

List price	N.A.
Suspension, front	telescopic fork
Suspension, rear	swinging arm
Tire, front	3.50-19
Tire, rear	4.00-18
Brake, front, diameter, width, in.	11.5, 1.75
Engine, type	dohc vertical Twin
Bore x stroke, in., mm	3.15 x 2.91, 80 x 74
Piston displacement, cu. in., cc	45.4, 743
Compression ratio	8.4:1
Claimed bhp @ rpm	63 @ 6500
Claimed torque @ rpm, lb.-ft.,	50.0
Carburetion	(2) 30mm Solex Mikuni
Ignition	battery, coil
Oil system	wet sump
Oil capacity, pt.	6.3
Fuel capacity, U.S. gal.	3.5
Recommended fuel	regular/premium
Starting system	electric, kick
Lighting system	12V alternator
Air filtration	fiber screen
Clutch	multi-disc, wet
Final drive	single-row chain

Gear ratios, overall:1	
5th	5.28
4th	6.05
3rd	7.18
2nd	8.58
1st	13.59
Wheelbase, in.	57.5
Seat height, in.	31.7
Seat width, in.	11.5
Handlebar width, in.	30.0
Footpeg height, in.	13.0
Ground clearance, in.	6.0 (at side stand)
Curb weight (w/half-tank fuel), lb.	520
Weight bias, front/rear, percent	45.5/54.5
Test weight (fuel and rider), lb.	680
Computed top speed in gears (@ 7000 rpm), mph:	
5th	101
4th	87
3rd	74
2nd	62
1st	39
Mph/1000 rpm, top gear	14.4
Engine revolutions/mile, top gear	4165
Piston speed (@ 7000 rpm), ft./min.	3393
Lb./hp with (160 lb. rider)	10.8

comparator converts the reading to a piece or "bit" of warning information only if the psi drops below the lower acceptable limit. Readout: valve job. If no readout at all: wait and we'll run it through the machine again at the next maintenance period.

In eliminating the progressive reading, you preclude the astute borderline diagnoses possible for a clever mechanic. However, it is debatable how useful a clever mechanic is. If he tells you that your cylinder pressure was 127 psi and although the bike is running okay now, you'll need a valve job in 3000 miles, is he really telling you anything you are going to act upon? I doubt it, unless of course you are an absolute perfectionist. Like most people, you'll let it slide for several weeks until you absolutely need it.

Much better for most people that they receive a cut and dried absolutist shmear from a computer for a ten-dollar bill than a terse, secretive check from a disinterested tune-up man at two or three times the price.

Indeed, when the inputs to the computer console reach a certain number, the console may be programmed to deliver quite sophisticated gradations of advice to the machine owner. For instance, combine comparator interpretations of dwell angle, plug voltage and fuel mixture to deduce the extent and cost of a proposed tune-up.

The major expense to the consumer is the inclusion of all these sensing devices on the motorcycle. Whether or not it is worthwhile depends on several things: Cost of installation versus cost of the machine to be sold. Type of machine: Is it

Wiring for Yamaha's brake lining light is strung along the swinging arm and into the hub underneath the brake arm.

INNOVATIVE PROTOTYPE

The TX750 handles quite well for a machine of its weight. The frame is based on the excellent double cradle frame that houses Yamaha's two-stroke 350 roadster and helps make it one of the best handling bikes you can buy. But even with the excellent frame, Yamaha must design excellent suspension to overcome the heavings created by 520 lb.

At the front end, they've done quite well with a set of double damping forks styled in the Ceriani tradition. At the rear, the rebound damping is inadequate and thus you feel slight amounts of unexpected wiggling over rough surfaces.

There is a trace of designed-in tendency to straighten when the bike is pitched hard into a short radius turn. It can be overcome well enough to move the bike around fast, and is not as noticeable in high-speed bends. It remains there as a safety factor for the novice rider—to prevent him from destroying a fifteen hundred dollar investment while rounding a 30 mph corner on the way to the drugstore. Some people won't like this trait completely, but they only have to tolerate it at up to 40 mph or so.

The hydraulically actuated front disc brake is an absolute necessity on this machine and seems reasonably adequate for the 750's weight and its intended usage. Its pads are double acting, which allows more rigid mounting of the calipers. In a single-caliper disc brake assembly, the mounting arm must have a certain amount of give to allow the stationary brake puck to center itself with the rotation of the disc.

A double-acting puck system, being self-centering with a rigid mounting, helps prevent either puck from dragging on the disc and reduces feedback of any distortions or flaws in the disc itself. In certain instances, it may dampen all or part of the high frequency oscillations that cause disc brakes to squeal.

Yamaha apparently thinks that some TX750 riders will want even more brake than the present set-up provides, as the left fork leg has been provided with all the necessary protrusions and holes to mount a mirror image of the brake already there. So if you want the feeling that the hand of God has reached out to pull you down almost instantaneously, Yamaha has left you the option.

While all these mechanical niceties are appealing, and make for a fine machine for touring or freeway commuting, the most devastating innovation on Yamaha's new bike may have to do with the little three-light idiot panel you can see next to the handlebars. It may seem like a gimmick, this panel which tells you about your oil pressure, taillight and brake lining condition, but it isn't.

In effect, that panel opens a new era in motorcycling—the era of diagnostics. Much has been said about this new vehicular science, which promises a quick way to diagnose the source of many actual or potential mechanical ills. In a way, it is much more earthshaking than the fact that Yamaha has finally civilized the vertical Twin, so Yamaha's "diagnostic panel" receives full treatment in the adjoining article. ◖O◗

Plug-in terminal for VW's system handles 150 bits of information, but is small enough for motorcycle application.

COMPUTERIZED SERVICING?

the sort of bike that is primarily owner-maintained? Number of miles that a machine like this is ridden: If the annual mileage figure is low, then there is not much value in an electric sensor readout for long-term maintenance items.

The choice of items to be measured must be made carefully. Furthermore, it is extremely important that there be a consensus among manufacturers on what constitutes a proper plug-in diagnostic system. Having each manufacturer develop his own system with total disregard for the others is to invite chaos in the service industry and resentment at both the rider and dealer level.

The introduction of the VW system to the automobile world has posed the same problem, which was the subject of a recent national meeting of engineers and government agency people in San Francisco. By encouraging a cross-breeding and exchange of ideas the government hopes to extract the maximum possible benefit from this new science.

The benefit is there, to be sure, for all you have to do is figure how much labor it would cost you to have a Yamaha mechanic dismount your rear wheel and check the brake lining. The labor charge would just about cover the cost of materials used for Yamaha's new sensor.

To me, that's progress. ◖O◗

YAMAHA TX750

Smooth, Fast, Easy Riding. This Is The Twin That Runs Like A Four.

WITH ALL the recent excitement about the many multi-cylinder motorcycles that are generally available today, the tried and true standby of many motorcycle fans has fallen into a back seat position. We're speaking, of course, about the vertical Twin, one of the most popular mounts for the sporting motorcyclist of just a few years ago. The vertical Twin combined  many of the attributes sought after by the true enthusiast: sleek styling, light weight and spirited performance.

But the vertical Twin had some faults, too, that just couldn't be tolerated by some motorcyclists. A vertical Twin has its pistons in one of two configurations: a 360-deg. crankshaft arrangement with the pistons rising and falling together, or the 180-deg. crank (made popular by Honda) with the pistons opposed in motion. Regardless of the layout, the vertical Twin has always suffered from a high level of vibration stemming from the engine design.

Heavy counterbalancing is required in a 360-deg. crankshaft layout because the pistons rise and fall together. But the damping of vibration is left primarily to heavy counterbalancing of the flywheel assembly which is only partially successful. The 180-deg. crankshaft arrangement is difficult to make smooth because of eccentric vibration patterns created by the design and because of the unequal firing impulses. Engine mounting methods and positions in the frame also influence the level of vibration to a great extent.

Until the emergence of the Yamaha TX750 the rider had to suffer varying degrees of vibration in a vertical Twin. A notable exception to this is the Norton Commando's "Isolastic" engine/transmission mounting method, which isolates the vibration from the frame. Own any other vertical Twin, and you just sit there and put up with it.

But even though the multi-cylinder mania appears to be taking over, there are many motorcyclists who know and appreciate the relative mechanical simplicity of a vertical Twin, the smaller number of moving parts to wear out and give

trouble, and who just plain enjoy the aura of riding a Twin. Yamaha has been primarily thought of as a manufacturer of two-cycle motorcycles, but the introduction of the XS-series ohc vertical Twins showed that its expertise wasn't limited to the two-cycle engine. The XS-series machines suffered from many of the ailments of any four-stroke machine of that design, too, but they've been getting better.

Rather than redesign its XS-series machine into a multi-cylinder arrangement, Yamaha went a step farther in the design and refinement of the vertical Twin. And in most respects it has been enormously successful. The sporting character of the Twin is still there, but refinements such as electric starting, mechanical silence and a comfortable ride with almost no vibration make the bike much easier to live with for the less hardy sportsman or the long distance touring rider.

The TX750 engine is similar to most Italian and Japanese four-stroke Twins in that it employs a horizontally-split crankcase assembly. With this design there are fewer joints through which oil can leak; and transmission servicing, should it be required, is much more easily accomplished. Four main bearings support the crankshaft and the two short and strong connecting rods ride on plain bearings at the crank journals for silent running and high load carrying capabilities. An endless, single-row chain runs from the center of the crankshaft over a series of rollers and dampers to drive the single overhead camshaft. Four short, finger-type rocker arms transmit the motion of the cam lobes to the valves in an extremely quiet and efficient manner.

Conventional three-ring pistons cram the fuel/air mixture into relatively shallow combustion chambers which are curiously sculptured to permit the most efficient burning possible. But even with efficient burning, there is some gas which is blown by the piston rings, polluting the oil in the crankcase. This blow-by is also discharged into the atmosphere. To fight the phenomenon, an automotive-type PCV valve using a reed valve and the engine's air cleaner is utilized successfully, although the amount of unburned HC is nowhere near that of an automobile. The vapors from the crankcase are then directed back into the carburetor inlets to be more completely burned.

But the most interesting aspect of the TX750's engine is the "omni-phase" balancer which nestles in a cavity beneath and slightly to the rear of the crankshaft. This balancer consists of two counter-rotating weights which are driven by a single chain from the crankshaft. One weight resembles a T-shaped flywheel, and the other is much smaller and passes very close to the "open" part of the T-shaped wheel, although it is rotating in the opposite direction. The smaller flywheel is used to obviate the turning force (moment) of the larger one.

The "omni-phase" balancer almost makes the need for more cylinders to balance out vibration superfluous, as its amplitude matches the amplitude of the main crankshaft and theoretically they cancel each other out. As with any mechanical device there is some vibration, but the almost total

YAMAHA

"Omni-phase" balancer weights are chain driven from the crankshaft...

...and nestle beneath the engine in this cavity.

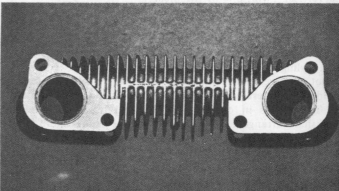

Cast aluminum exhaust manifold features a built-in balance tube.

In spite of the large displacement engine, the TX750 is reasonably narrow.

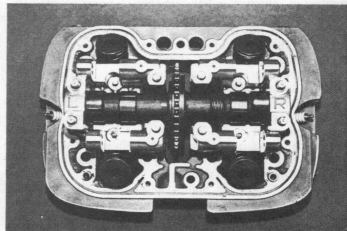

lack of it makes the rider think he is riding a four-stroke Four. And there are no lateral effects like a horizontally opposed Twin when the throttle is blipped open, either.

The use of chains inside the power producing part of the engine also contributes to the relative mechanical silence of the TX750. There is little more than the burble of the exhaust and even fainter ticking of the tappets to hint that the big Twin is running.

In harmony with the low mechanical noise is the mellow, pleasing tone of the twin megaphone-shaped mufflers and the low carburetor inlet noise level. Only at really large throttle openings does the TX750 begin to bellow, but not objectionally.

The TX750 transmission has been borrowed *in toto* from the highly successful XS-2 model and needs little criticism. All-indirect ratio gears are slid back and forth along the mainshaft and layshaft by three girdling shifter forks, and usually provided the rider with crisp, positive gear changes. When the engine was hot, shifting was a little unsure in feel, but this condition should cure itself when the machine is completely broken in.

With a rather low (high numerically) overall gear ratio of 5.09:1 the five-speed transmission seemed like frosting on a cake instead of a necessity. A whopping 56.6 lb.-ft. of torque is available at 6000 rpm, but the curve feels almost ruler flat from as low as 2000 rpm, making it unnecessary to row the gear lever back and forth to keep the engine rpm up.

The one point in the drive train which seems to need attention is the clutch. When hot the clutch would drag slightly, making it impossible to select neutral after stopping for a traffic light. Many experienced riders merely snick the machine into neutral just before stopping to prevent the clutch from heating up while stopped. This technique worked well in this case, but it shouldn't be necessary. However, there was very little clutch slip at the drag strip and clean shifts were the rule if you pressed firmly on the gear pedal. Clutch lever pressure is a little on the harsh side, but that's the price one pays for no slippage.

Even though the teeth on the crankshaft and on the clutch wheel are of the spur (straight-cut) variety, they don't seem to add any noise to the engine. Spur gears are generally noisy, but are slightly more efficient in operation than helical cut gears. Springs inside the clutch hub smooth out the power impulses from the crankshaft at low rpm before they reach the transmission, and lessen the strain put on the gears and the rear chain. At low rpm there was a hint of drive train roughness, due mostly to the widely spaced firing intervals of a four-stroke Twin.

The Yamaha TX750 is just what Yamaha designed it to be—a lush touring machine, not a "stoplight-to-stoplight" racer's delight, in spite of some rather good quarter-mile acceleration times. The physical largeness and weight of the machine have helped the designers come up with a really comfortable package for the tourer. Wide, comfortably shaped handlebars, a wide, soft seat (which is a bit harder at the extreme forward point) and just the right distance between them and the footpegs contribute to a very comfortable ride. Control location was deemed excellent by all our staff members, and the rear passenger seating position was acclaimed by all (birds) who sampled it.

There are some shortcomings in the panel of idiot lights just below the speedometer and tachometer dials. The oil pressure warning is on the left, a new light which warns when the rear brake lining reaches a specified thickness is in the center, and what we feel is a completely useless one is located on the right. This latter one is a stoplight warning light which comes on

lad, it makes the rider think he is riding a four-stroke Four, and there are no lateral effects like a horizontally opposed Twin when the throttle is shipped open, either.

The use of chain drive the power producing part of the engine also contributes to the relative mechanical silence of the TX750. There is little more than the burble of the exhaust and even faster fle-up of the tappets to hint that the big Twin is running.

In harmony with the low mechanical noise is the mellow, pleasing tone of the twin megaphone-shaped mufflers and the [...]

every time you activate the brakes.

This is in reverse to the standard logic of a warning system. A person usually associates a red light with some sort of trouble, and having this light come on frequently in traffic, when everything is OK, is distinctly annoying.

The real fireworks are reserved for when the stoplight filiment burns out, at which time the corresponding idiot light begins flashing on and off relentlessly until you get things fixed. Or until you get wise and disconnect the idiot light.

Annoying, yes, but an introduction to Yamaha's new orientation to riding safety. Both the stoplight and brake lining wear indicators are provocative moves on Yamaha's part. We hope in coming years that the concepts implied in these gadgets mature into a technician-oriented diagnostic system, rather than becoming a gleam in a Federal bureaucrat's eye.

The TX750 shows Yamaha's concern in providing the heavy machine with brakes to match its performance. Physically small, the front brake caliper is an efficient double acting unit which requires very little pressure from the adjustable lever to give safe, sure stops. The adjustment on the lever allows the rider to vary the point where the front brake begins working, a boon to riders with short fingers. As with most disc brake setups, there was not a hint of fade.

The rear brake is somewhat less certain in feel, but boasts a drum diameter of nearly 8 in. and a brake lining width of 1.85 in. Hauling a heavy motorcycle down from high speeds repeatedly is a difficult job, but stopping the TX750 was easy and safe.

Aside from the weight, which comes from such extras as electric starting and beefy structural components, the main complaint we had about the Yamaha was in the handling department. Ride smoothness is very good, but this smoothness comes at the expense of inhibited cornering characteristics. Front fork travel is good and the forks themselves do a good job of soaking up the bumps, but they are too soft for really precise steering at high speeds in turns. The same goes for the rear units, which exhibit too little rebound damping and make the machine "pogo" in fast, bumpy turns.

The TX750 is really not a sporting rider's machine like most vertical Twins, it's a luxurious tourer. General overall finish is what we've come to expect from Yamaha, with the traditional unevenness of welding on the frame adding the only sore spot. Bright, chrome-plated fenders, evenly applied paintwork and brightly polished aluminum set off the machine. Aluminum alloy wheel rims, manufactured by Dido in Japan, also add a touch of class and marginally reduce unsprung weight.

Electrical components are first rate and lighting controls are within easy reach. All wiring is neatly routed and tucked in to avoid damage, and the lights are more than adequate for high speed touring at night.

Some of the features we liked about the TX750 were the locking gas tank cap which is unlocked with the ignition key; the large, easy-to-read instruments, and the cast aluminum exhaust manifold which contains a balance tube. A vane-type steering damper nestles neatly beneath the lower triple-clamp and the cover surrounding the oil tank is vented to allow additional cooling of the oil supply on fast runs on a hot day. The TX750 also has a bracket to firmly lock your helmet strap under the seat.

In general, the TX750 is a real gem. The engine is the most original design of its configuration in decades, and it pays off in superlative smoothness at any speed. Yet it retains the simplicity and ease of maintenance of two cylinders.

If you are a man of the highways, take a good look at this one.

YAMAHA TX750

SPECIFICATIONS

List price	N.A.
Suspension, front	telescopic fork
Suspension, rear	swinging arm
Tire, front	3.50-19
Tire, rear	4.00-18
Brake, front, diameter x width, in.	(2)11.5 x 1.75
Brake, rear, diameter x width, in.	7.8 x 1.85
Total brake swept area, sq. in.	104
Brake loading, lb./sq. in. (with 160-lb. load)	6.7
Engine, type	sohc vertical Twin
Bore x stroke, in., mm	3.15 x 2.91, 80 x 74
Piston displacement, cu. in., cc	45.4, 743
Compression ratio	8.4:1
Claimed bhp @ rpm	63 @ 6500
Claimed torque @ rpm, lb.-ft.,	56.6 @ 6000
Carburetion	(2) 38mm Solex CV
Ignition	battery & coil
Oil system	dry sump, twin pumps
Oil capacity, pt.	6.0
Fuel capacity, U.S. gal.	3.7
Recommended fuel	premium
Starting system	electric; kick, folding crank
Lighting system	12V alternator
Air filtration	dry foam
Clutch	multi-disc, wet
Primary drive	spur gear
Final drive	single-row chain
Gear ratios, overall:1	
5th	5.09
4th	5.83
3rd	6.92
2nd	8.45
1st	13.10
Wheelbase, in.	58
Seat height, in.	32
Seat width, in.	11
Handlebar width, in.	31
Footpeg height, in.	12.5
Ground clearance, in.	6
Curb weight (w/half-tank fuel), lb.	514
Weight bias, front/rear, percent	46/54
Test weight (fuel and rider), lb.	664

TEST CONDITIONS

Air temperature, degrees F	86
Humidity, percent	51
Barometric pressure, in. hg.	30.23
Altitude above mean sea level, ft.	50
Wind velocity, mph	12-15
Strip alignment, relative wind:	

PERFORMANCE

Top speed (actual @ 7067 rpm), mph	105
Computed top speed in gears (@ 7000 rpm), mph:	
5th	104
4th	91
3rd	77
2nd	63
1st	40
Mph/1000 rpm, top gear	14.87
Engine revolutions/mile, top gear	4035
Piston speed (@ 7000 rpm), ft./min.	3395
Lb./hp (160-lb. load)	10.70
Fuel consumption, mpg	40
Speedometer error:	
50 mph indicated, actually	45
60 mph indicated, actually	56
70 mph indicated, actually	65
Braking distance:	
from 30 mph, ft.	34
from 60 mph, ft.	144
Acceleration, zero to:	
30 mph, sec.	3.7
40 mph, sec.	4.3
50 mph, sec.	5.2
60 mph, sec.	6.0
70 mph, sec.	7.2
80 mph, sec.	8.9
90 mph, sec.	11.4
100 mph, sec.	16.9
Standing one-eighth mile, sec.	8.62
terminal speed, mph	79.36
Standing one-quarter mile, sec.	13.78
terminal speed, mph	94.33

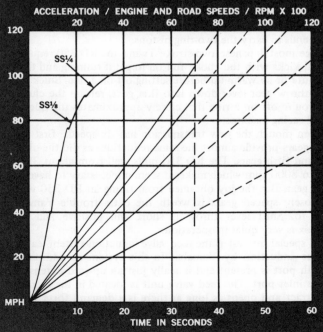

ACCELERATION / ENGINE AND ROAD SPEEDS / RPM X 100

TIME IN SECONDS

start wind

■ THE NEW YAMAHA RD 350 might well be termed the brother of the giant killer if it were compared to its stablemate, the TR3. Racing versions of the RD 350 have successfully trounced machines over twice their size in AMA Class C competition for the past several years with such regularity that you know it couldn't be a mistake.

Many features of the new RD 350 have come as a direct result of Yamaha's participation in road racing, both in the United States and abroad, proving that there is truth in the adage "racing improves the breed."

The RD 350 is a cafe racer's delight with its slim, sleek styling, disc brake on the front wheel and a closely-spaced six-speed transmission. It also appeals to the daily commuter who rides his motorcycle back and forth to work. Its light weight and nimble handling characteristics make it an ideal vehicle for combating the traffic jams found in so many of today's cities.

Or take the RD 350 out on a favorite stretch of hilly, winding road where the six-speed transmission and powerful front disc brake can be used to their fullest and you'll find a race-bred motorcycle in a street machine's clothing.

Here is where we find out what a motorcycle can do. Accelerate rapidly to a certain speed, decelerate by use of the brakes, swoop through a series of turns at a good angle of lean without dragging the side or center stand. This is where the RD 350 excels.

High speed turns exhibited the bike's near neutral handling characteristics with little tendency to oversteer when the power was applied. It had no tendency to plow or turn in on itself in slow turns. It felt as though the Yamaha was on rails, the rear wheel faithfully following the line taken by the front wheel. These are the same fine characteristics we found on the R5 that we tested a couple of years ago.

Aside from the reed valve induction system and the six-speed transmission the RD 350 is almost a carbon copy of last year's R5D. The narrow crankshaft assembly is supported by four hefty ball bearings and a labyrinth seal separates the two crank chambers. Roller bearings support the connecting rods at the bottom and needle bearings are employed at the small ends to carry the two-ring pistons.

Like most Japanese two-stroke Twins, the RD 350 requires several kicks with the choke full on to get it running and then a minute or so warm-up before setting off on a ride. Snick the short-throw gear lever down into first gear, release the clutch and you're off on a ride that closely approximates the ride on a road racing machine.

Even though the new transmission has six speeds, first and sixth gears provide almost the same reductions as did the older first and fifth gears. The RD 350 pulls well from about 3500 rpm to 8000 rpm which makes it seem unnecessary to have an extra gear. But the joy obtained from riding an RD 350 with its closely spaced gears is worth the extra trouble Yamaha went to. Shift lever throw is short and positive and the gearbox is very quiet in operation.

Of special interest is the reed valve induction system, called Torque Induction by Yamaha. In this system an additional seventh port is present and is really just an upward extension of the inlet port. The reed valve unit is located in the original inlet tract and opens as long as there is a demand for a fresh fuel/air charge, hence there is less chance of fuel being wasted by too great a throttle opening in relation to the engine's rpm or from blow-back through the carburetor because of too low >

YAMAHA RD350

Reed Valve Induction, A Disc Front
Brake And A Six-Speed Gearbox Add Class
To An Already Superb Machine.

an engine rpm for a particular throttle opening.

Peak horsepower of the RD 350 is up to 39 bhp as opposed to 36 bhp for last year's R5C. The RD 350 also got slightly better gas mileage than the first R5.

Oil for lubricating the engine's internals comes from a tank located under the right hand side of the seat and is metered by the Autolube pump. This pump works off the end of the crankshaft and meters the engine's oil according to the crankshaft rpm and the throttle opening. As the throttle is opened when climbing a hill the pump's output is increased, but when cruising on level ground or descending a hill, the pump's delivery is cut down accordingly to keep the engine from loading up with unburned oil.

Even though the RD 350 is not what we would call a full-sized motorcycle, the riding position proved quite comfortable to all our staff members for a short ride around town, but really more comfortable to the shorter ones.

If we were grading the suspension, it would get an "A" for roadholding and a "B" for comfort. The seat is a little hard and the front forks and rear suspension members are too firm for the Cadillac ride. But it's hard to combine this kind of handling with armchair comfort, and this firmness adds to the feeling of confidence you get when flicking the RD 350 from side to side in an exciting set of bends. Stability is first rate and the rebound damping of both the front forks and the rear shocks seemed just right.

The excellent brakes were also part of the RD 350's charm. Although greatly overshadowed by the fadeless stopping power of the 10.5 in. disc on the front wheel, the rear drum brake performed well and only faded slightly during our 60-0 mph stopping tests. The front brake features a double acting caliper unit in which both pads are forced into the disc to perform the braking operation, rather than the earlier design where only one pad moves and the caliper floats into alignment when the brake is used.

A handsome instrument panel encases the tachometer, speedometer, turn signal indicators, high beam indicator light and a light that comes on when the brake light is activated. This lamp merely tells the rider when his brake light isn't working and although we felt it was annoying at first, we realize that is is an important safety feature. An "off-run-off" switch is located on the right handlebar and a flick in either direction will stop the engine should trouble arise.

Much of the RD 350's sure-footedness comes from the double cradle frame, which bears a strong resemblance to the TR series racing machines. Additional bracing and gussets in highly stressed areas like the steering head and swinging arm pivot points aid in making the RD 350 the handler that it is.

We liked the appearance of the engine/transmission unit which is finished in a dull black with the fin edges and heightened portions highly polished to accent the classic design lines. This dull black finish also serves to dissipate heat and adds an air of authority to the unit.

We also liked the vane-type steering damper which fits below the bottom triple clamp. It adds just the right amount of drag to help steady the front end when traversing bumpy corners at speed.

Another nice touch is the locking gas filler cap which is unlocked by the ignition key. This will keep the curious little guy down the street from dumping a handful of gravel in your gas tank when you won't take him for a ride!

The RD 350 fills the bill in many respects. Few are the enthusiasts who would want to journey from coast to coast on one, but the short haul commuter and the inveterate cafe racer will love it.

The RD 350 has its parallel in the automotive world-the

Datsun 240Z. Like that popular medium-priced sports car, it offers a combination of two winning features: devastating performance and excitement at a moderate price, and the seemingly contradictory promise of appliance-like reliability.

The enthusiast who wants a taste of that elusive racing quality without the more odious tasks of maintenance which sometimes seem to go with it would do well to try the RD 350. ◙

YAMAHA RD350

SPECIFICATIONS

List price	$839
Suspension, front	telescopic fork
Suspension, rear	swinging arm
Tire, front	3.00-18
Tire, rear	3.50-18
Brake, front, diameter x width, in.	(2) 10.5 x 1.85
Brake, rear, diameter x width, in.	7.08 x 1.37
Total brake swept area, sq. in.	86
Brake loading, lb./sq. in. with 160-lb. load	5.9
Engine, type	two-stroke Twin
Bore x stroke, in., mm	2.52 x 2.13, 64 x 54
Piston displacement, cu. in., cc	21.17, 347
Compression ratio	6.8:1 (corrected)
Claimed bhp @ rpm	39 @ 7500
Claimed torque @ rpm, lb.-ft.,	28.0 @ 7000
Carburetion	(2) Mikuni VM 28 SC
Ignition	coil & battery
Oil system	oil injection
Oil capacity, pt.	4.2
Fuel capacity, U.S. gal.	3.2
Recommended fuel	premium
Starting system	kick, folding crank
Lighting system	12V alternator
Air filtration	treated dry paper
Clutch	multi-disc, wet
Primary drive	helical gear
Final drive	single-row chain
Gear ratios, overall:1	
6th	6.00
5th	6.80
4th	7.96
3rd	10.08
2nd	13.60
1st	19.67
Wheelbase, in.	52.5
Seat height, in.	30
Seat width, in.	9.5
Handlebar width, in.	29
Footpeg height, in.	12
Ground clearance, in.	7.0
Curb weight (w/half-tank fuel), lb.	344
Weight bias, front/rear, percent	45/55
Test weight (fuel and rider), lb.	475
Mileage at completion of test	330

TEST CONDITIONS

Air temperature, degrees F	66
Humidity, percent	71
Barometric pressure, in. hg.	29.70
Altitude above mean sea level, ft.	50
Wind velocity, mph	4-6
Strip alignment, relative wind:	

PERFORMANCE

Top speed (actual @ 8000 rpm), mph	99
Computed top speed in gears (@8000 rpm), mph:	
6th	99
5th	87
4th	74
3rd	59
2nd	43
1st	30
Mph/1000 rpm, top gear	12.3
Engine revolutions/mile, top gear	4878
Piston speed (@8500 rpm), ft./min.	3010
Lb/hp (test wt.)	12.2
Fuel consumption, mpg	40
Speedometer error:	
50 mph indicated, actually	46
60 mph indicated, actually	56
70 mph indicated, actually	65
Braking distance:	
from 30 mph, ft.	29
from 60 mph, ft.	122
Acceleration, zero to:	
30 mph, sec.	2.9
40 mph, sec.	3.6
50 mph, sec.	4.7
60 mph, sec.	5.9
70 mph, sec.	7.1
80 mph, sec.	9.8
80 mph, sec.	14.4
Standing one-eighth mile, sec.	9.07
terminal speed, mph	78.05
Standing one-quarter mile, sec.	14.30
terminal speed, mph	89.82

ACCELERATION / ENGINE AND ROAD SPEEDS / RPM X 100

DIVERSITY OF engine design is a sound marketing idea, as it allows the consumer a wide choice of machines with the opportunity to maintain brand loyalty. For 1973, Yamaha has the edge. It not only produces several two-strokes and three four-stroke road burners, but has recently built a revolutionary twin-rotor Wankel-powered machine as well.

Patrons of the 19th Tokyo Motor Show were the first to view the RZ 201, as the new prototype is called. And, as the accompanying photos suggest, it is impossible to walk away unimpressed.

Unlike the Hercules Wankel CYCLE WORLD previewed in the January '71 issue, the RZ is of twin-rotor design with axis of rotation at a right angle to the direction of vehicle advance. This effectively eliminates the sideways torque reaction of machines with rotors or crankshafts that revolve at right angles to the direction of vehicle travel.

Besides lending itself well to chain drive to the rear wheel, the Yamaha approach enables the rotor chambers to be placed above the transmission package. This creates a unit of more or less conventional dimensions that is easily installed in a frame. In fact, the traditionally tall engine bays of two or four-stroke motorcycles need not be altered at all.

Contrast this with the Hercules. If its horizontal engine were a twin-rotor, the engine/transmission package would become too long to be practical.

For reasons of compactness, silence of operation, and reliability, Yamaha's Wankel is water-cooled. Also in the interest of reliability, Yamaha has invented CCR or charge cooled rotor lubrication. In this system, the fuel-air mixture from the carburetor is further mixed with oil for efficient cooling and lubrication of the rotors.

Proper cooling and lubrication is essential in a Wankel engine because the seal velocity on the chamber walls is rapid and temperatures on the portion of the wall where combustion occurs are much higher than in a conventional internal combustion engine.

Although mixing of oil and gas causes the Wankel to be an inherently dirty engine in terms of air pollution, the units respond better to air pollution control devices than do conventional engines. Wankel engines are not overly fussy about fuel, and this may give them the edge in future years.

In terms of air pollution, then, the Wankel is not the ultimate answer, even though it does have potential in this area of concern. So why did Yamaha choose a Wankel to power its latest superbike. Aside from being different, Wankel powerplants offer the four-stroke attribute of compression braking when the throttle is rolled off, they have broad power bands and they are generally smooth running.

Smoothness is inherent in the basic design. Every Wankel converts a series of separate combustion chamber explosions into rotary motion. In the Yamaha, there are two three-vaned rotors housed inside two oblong (epitrochoidal) chambers. Each rotor is subjected to three Otto cycles (intake, compression, combustion, exhaust) per revolution as it travels an eccentric path in the chamber.

The eccentric path introduces a certain vibration potential into the design, but because each rotor only revolves once for every three revolutions of the output shaft and because the eccentric path is small, vibration is minimal. Besides, the rotors are easily counter-balanced.

One may conclude, then, that the 68-bhp Yamaha will be both smooth and a capable performer. It combines the 59.4 in. wheelbase and girth of a

YAMAHA RZ 201 WANKEL

**Twin Rotors. Water-Cooling.
Disc Brakes Front And Rear.
Is This Tomorrow's
Superbike Today?**

touring machine with the power potential and style of a stoplight-to-stoplight GP bike. Add to this a five-speed transmission, disc brakes at both ends and electric starting, and you have a bike with incredible consumer appeal.

You'll not see this machine in 1973, as Yamaha must first investigate its marketing possibilities. When it comes, the R-Z should provide fascinating riding. ◨

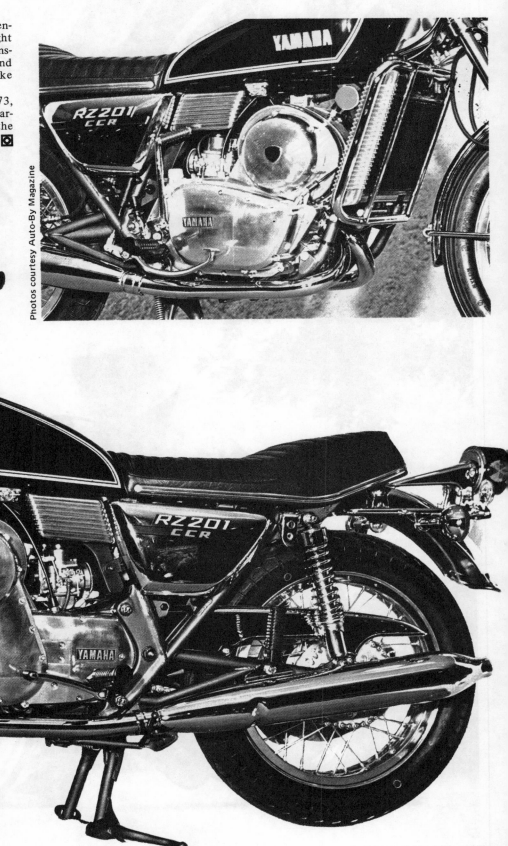

Photos courtesy Auto-By Magazine

nt end assembly houses all the rider's
trols. Fuel tank holds two quarts.
ering damper is from Honda.

A DIFFERENT APPROACH

The Bowers/Davis 650 Yamaha Lacks What Is Considered Essential On More Conventional Drag Machines/By D. Randy Riggs

WORKING IN Yamaha International Corporation's Snowmobile Racing Department has had its advantages for Mike Bowers and Rodger Davis. Rodger, as racing director, and Mike, as the head of technical research, have pooled the knowledge and experience gained with snowmobiles and applied it to their favorite hobby—motorcycle drag racing.

Both men have been involved with the drags for a number of years, competing with cars as well as bikes. Rodger presently holds a couple of NHRA records with a 350 Yamaha and has set marks at Bonneville and AHRA meets. Recently he has become involved with snowmobile grass drags, varying his experience even more. Rodger's reflexes are sharp, due to the extra practice and conditioning.

With much time spent together in the Snow-Mo racing division, Mike and Rodger began toying with some new ideas. Deep down inside both had an urge to build an all-out drag machine. Bower's thoughts went even farther. He wanted to build a 9-sec. two-stroke, and he had some new innovations tucked up his sleeve that he hoped would allow him to pull it off.

Both felt that the biggest loss in elapsed time during a quarter-mile acceleration run was during a shift and off the line with a hand actuated clutch. By eliminating the clutch and the gearbox you also eliminate many variables. The only question is, "What do you replace them with?" Here's where the snowmobile experience came in.

The team decided to try a torque converter from a 650 Yamaha snowmobile. At the same time, Bowers and Davis elected to use the engine attached to it. The engine had found its way into a motorcycle chassis in several experimental applications, so they felt it

Right side case contains flywheel/magneto, hand recoil starter.

wouldn't be too far out of the question.

Most motorcycle enthusiasts are not aware of the fact that Yamaha does indeed build a 650cc two-stroke engine. Many of the components are, in fact, identical to those found in certain models of Yamaha motorcycles. If the high horsepower that the Twin produced could be transferred through the torque converter and out to the rear wheel, Mike and Rodger knew they would have a winner.

First on the list of essentials was a proper chassis. The team went to Doug Schwerma and ordered one of his standard drag frames and the project was underway. The 8-lb. unit was handed over to Mike Harper of Victor Products in Temple City, Calif., who made up the necessary engine mounts and fashioned the front and rear axles, as well as the special self-centering rear wheel bearings.

For front suspension the team again looked to Yamaha. Forks came from an 80cc model, with a 125 machine donating its front brake and hub assembly.

Photos by Dave Gooley

The forks were modified somewhat by using the valve springs from a 650 Yamaha ohc four-stroke, instead of the stock internal fork coils. These, coupled with no oil whatsoever in the legs, contribute to 1.5-in. of suspension cushioning, quite sufficient for a drag strip surface.

Buchanan spokes tie up the 125 hub with a 2.00-18 Akront rim, which mounts a Dunlop road racing tire. To get a better roll on the lights, Davis installed an aluminum disc to the front wheel, as is common practice.

The steering head contains Yamaha bearings and races; fork crowns are stock Yamaha at the bottom and homemade stainless steel on the top. To help control any possible tank-slapping tendencies, a Honda steering damper was fitted and painted crinkle black to match the fork legs, top crown, and the engine cylinders and cases.

One of the first things you notice about the machine is the fine attention to detail and sanitary construction and finish. Nothing is left undone or un-
>

cared for. Every rivet, bolt or nut is either plated or buffed. Each wire or cable is routed precisely in position. Safety is built-in. It's as much a part of the machine as the engine, and was one of the team's main objectives.

The 2-qt. fuel tank was built by steel shoe man Ken Maeley. It's formed from anodized aluminum and nestles just behind the steering head between the frame rails. Normal, everyday pump gasoline is used at the present, since the bike competes in the NHRA G/Gas class.

Rodger steers with Webco clip-on bars that mount the control levers for both the front and rear brake assemblies. The right lever operates the cable actuated front brake, just like on most motorcycles. The left one is a bit out of the ordinary, however. Why? Have you ever seen a left hand hydraulic brake unit? Probably not. This is one of the few ever produced, made originally for a Yamaha snowmobile.

The master cylinder operates the rear brake, which is a Kelsey Hayes disc and caliper combination. Davis was quite particular about choosing his brakes and that's mainly why he used stoppers at both wheels. If he were to lose his rear brake for any reason and had no front unit to back it up, he'd be in big trouble at 135 mph. The torque converter would do nothing to slow the machine, unlike a transmission with which you could at least shift down.

For traction Bowers and Davis went to an M&H drag slick, in which they normally carry about 12 to 13 lb. of air for most strips. The 4.00-18 tire fits on an Akront rim. Sheet metal screws run through the rim and into the sidewall of the tire to secure the tire to the rim without danger of it slipping and tearing out the valve stem.

The 68-in. wheelbase machine gets its go from a very unusual power and drive

combination. To date it's been sufficient enough to carry Rodger and the bike to a very fast 10.009 e.t. with a speed of 134.86 mph. If that sounds slow compared to the nine flats turned in by some of the Harleys, remember this thing runs in G/Gas. The record for the class is in the neighborhood of 10.80, so you can see the Bowers/Davis bike is trick.

The Yammy mill actually displaces 643cc and produces right around 100 horsepower. You'd probably be a non-believer until you watched this thing go. It's enough to temporarily displace brain fluid. Crankcase halves separate horizontally and house a sturdy looking crank assembly. The right side of the crankshaft mounts the Yamaha magneto system and flywheel. The left side is more interesting. This is where we find the unique drive system—the torque converter.

The primary clutch unit is attached directly to the crank. This unit has a spool that the drive belt runs around. On the end of the spool is the actual clutch assembly, a group of contracting discs that change when engine rpm is increased. The drive belt is toothed to mesh with corresponding grooves in the spool assemblies.

The belt runs from the primary clutch assembly to the secondary clutch assembly, which works just the opposite. Its discs expand, rather than contract, and the end result is a change in the overall gear ratio from 0:1 to 1:1 at top speed. By making certain adjustments, the ratios can be made to change at different rpms to suit different engines. Presently, the engine develops its power at 8000 rpm, so the clutches are set up to change when the unit reaches that peak.

To transfer the power from the secondary unit to the rear drive chain, a jackshaft was built. It rests in mounts built into the frame and carries a primary sprocket on its end. That in turn connects to the chain which continues

to the rear sprocket and the linkup is completed. As complicated as the unit may sound, it is actually very simple, and very efficient.

The rider has no worries about a missed shift or feathering the clutch off the line. Rodger simply watches the lights, twists the throttle when the light goes green, and steers—that's it!

The team had Tom Rightmeyer build a magnesium cover for the entire assembly, and even though it looks large, it only weighs 1.5 lb. Items such as this contribute to an overall weight of just 186 lb., probably the lightest 650 drag machine ever.

Another unusual item is the method of supplying fuel to the cylinders. Two 50mm Keihin diaphragm carburetors are actually a carb-injection system. They work off of crankcase impulses and deliver fuel at an alarming rate! They have no floats of any kind and are not affected by varying temperatures. The starting drill is simple: turn on the petcocks, hold a hand over one of the carb intakes, and pull the hand recoil starter. Just like a lawnmower!

The machine is allowed to idle and warm up. If any revving is needed, the rear wheel must first be raised off the ground; otherwise, the bike will take off. It's just like riding a mini-bike with a centrifugal clutch, only faster.

Finishing off the pacesetting machine is a Schwerma seat and an eyecatching racing orange color accented with gold touches. Pipes by Wheelsmith Engineering of Santa Ana not only help with the performance but fit in with the quality of the remainder of the bike.

The team of Bowers and Davis have come up with a truly innovative machine. The word is that they're working on another. We can only imagine what that will be like.... ◨

With cover removed, primary and secondary clutch units are visible. Bowers replaces V-belt occasionally.

View of jackshaft assembly and mounts. Indentation holes in spool are for balancing.

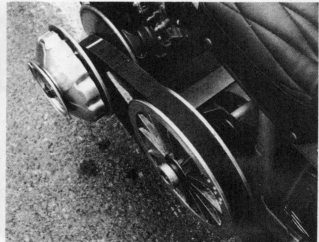

■ UNTIL THE introduction of the XS-1 650cc sohc vertical Twin in 1970, Yamaha's entire production was of two-stroke motorcycles. These ranged in size from the 50cc Single to the 350cc Twin, and there were models which suited the commuter, the trail rider and the sports oriented street rider just fine. But the long distance touring buff was left without a suitable mount.

The XS-1 was a step in the right direction, but it suffered from one of the shortcomings of most four-stroke vertical Twins: vibration. Yamaha corrected this, however, with the introduction of the TX750, and the subject of this test, the super trick TX500.

We realize that the word "trick" is usually reserved for modified machines, but in the case of the TX500 it is equally appropriate. Here's why. The 500cc vertical Twin that powers the TX has twin overhead camshafts, four valves per cylinder, an electric starter and an Omni-phase balancer to control vibration. That alone is enough to place the machine in the trick category, but there's more. There is a disc brake up front

and somehow Yamaha engineers have fit all this in a machine not much larger than their RD350 two-stroke.

At first glance, in fact, the TX500 looks very similar to the Yamaha RD350 Twin. The seat, gasoline tank and headlights look very much the same, and once aboard, the seating positions are very similar, too. Not surprisingly, the handling characteristics are also similar, although the TX500 is several pounds heavier, tipping the scales at 433 lb. ready to go with a half tank of fuel.

Starting the TX500 is decidedly simple. Switch on the ignition, close the choke lever, press the starter button and the engine bursts to life almost immediately. Soon it settles down to a smooth idle, with very little mechanical noise. After a brief warm-up, low gear can be selected and one of the smoothest rides on a machine of this configuration can be begun.

The ordinarily round steel clutch plates are flattened somewhat between the outer third of each plate and these are installed with the flattened portions 120-deg. apart to eliminate the rattle when the clutch lever is withdrawn. Seven of these plain plates and eight plates with a bonded on lining give plenty of total area to prevent clutch slip, even under hard acceleration.

YAMAHA TX500

Yamaha Laid Down A Mandamus To Its Engineers: Build Us A Four-Stroke 500 Twin That Charms . . . And They Did!

Spacing between the transmission's five ratios is close to ideal and shifting effort is held to a minimum by a precisely machined shifting drum and shifter fork arrangement. Gearshift lever travel is short and positive, adding to the snug feeling of the machine.

The engine unit itself is fairly compact considering the number of components inside. Following racing automobile practice, all the bearings in the power producing section are plain bearings. The crankshaft rides on three plain main bearings, the connecting rod big end bearings have babbitt-type inserts and the small end bearings which support the piston pins are plain bushes. Even the twin overhead camshafts, which are steel, ride in plain bearings in the aluminum supports.

Ball bearings support the transmission shafts, however, and the oil for both the engine and transmission is circulated by an Eaton-type variable displacement pump with twin rotors to ensure a copious supply of oil to both lubricate and cool the moving parts of the engine.

One of the first things you notice about the TX500 is the very low vibration level. This is brought about by the use of the Omni-phase balancer which has counterweights to cancel out the main flywheels' imbalance, but unlike the TX750,

only one shaft with two bobweights is used. There is still some vibration, but it is of such low magnitude that it is not bothersome at any speed above 2500 rpm right up to the 9000 rpm red-line.

Rakishly upswept mufflers emit only a whisper, engine noise is very low and intake roar when the throttle is opened wide is not objectionable. At a steady 70 mph the loudest noise you hear is the wind rushing past your helmet!

Controls are all well placed, with the handlebar switches clearly labeled to avoid confusion. The left hand switches are the horn button, turn signal switch and the headlight high/low beam control. The right hand controls are the headlight on/off switch, and electric starter button and an off/run/off switch to stop the engine in the unlikely event of a throttle malfunction. Unlike some motorcycles we've tested lately, all the switches are within easy reach of the rider's thumbs, and worked perfectly every time.

The instrument panel contains a large speedometer and tachometer, nicely illuminated at night by a soft green glow. The non-glare resistant glass lenses, however, reflect sunlight right into the rider's eyes during the day. A stoplight indicator and an oil pressure light are red in color and can be clearly seen at all times, but the yellow turn signal indicators are

TX500

difficult to see on a sunny day. The ignition switch is located where it should be: right in the middle of the instrument panel and the key not only serves to turn on the ignition, it also unlocks the gasoline filler cap, the seat and the steering head locks.

As mentioned earlier, the TX500 handles very much like its smaller brother, the RD350. Fairly low handlebars contribute to the nearly perfect seating position and foot peg location to make the machine a joy to ride around town and at a fast clip on swervy roads. The only part of the layout we could find fault with was the seat, which is too hard (from lack of sufficient padding) for extended periods of cruising in a straight line. Oddly enough, we received no complaints from our passengers who spent as much as two hours on their half of the seat.

Of interest to the sporting rider are the brakes. The rear is a conventional drum type which, in spite of its rather small size, is very powerful and highly resistant to fade. The front disc brake is superlative in operation. A handlebar-mounted master cylinder is acted upon directly by the front brake lever and forces the brake fluid down to a double-acting caliper unit which forces the pads against the brake disc without having to have a floating, self-aligning caliper.

There are lugs already cast into the left hand fork leg to mount a similar caliper to the other side for those riders who prefer even more braking power than the standard setup. We feel that the single disc is more than adequate and even after more than half a dozen panic stops from 60 mph during our braking tests we didn't note any appreciable fade. In addition, the disc brake components are lighter in weight than a drum brake with similar stopping power, reducing the unsprung weight which so seriously affects handling.

Also important to the handling qualities of a motorcycle are the suspension components. The front forks provide 5.5-in. of travel and even though they are sprung on the soft side for comfort, both compression and rebound damping are adjusted to provide good roadholding characteristics, even over rough pavement. The rear suspension components are getting better on Japanese machines, but with the springs in their lowest (softest) position, the machine would wallow slightly in fast turns. Jacking the spring adjustment up all the way stiffened up the ride a little but made the machine more stable when blasting through bumpy turns. Also, with the springs in the softest position there was the feeling that the bike was hinged in the middle under difficult turn conditions, but this feeling almost disappeared when the springs were stiffened up.

On a warm afternoon we began an extended trip which

included about 50 miles of freeway riding. The front forks were sensitive enough to absorb the small ripples where the sections of concrete are joined, and the grooved pavement stretches on some California freeways didn't cause the machine to wander.

A small complaint we had regarding the difficulty of riding the machine smoothly was directly related to the push-pull throttle arrangement. Two cables emerge from opposite sides of the throttle control with one pulling the throttle open and the other pulling it closed when the throttle grip is turned forward. In theory, this arrangement works fine; but even with careful adjustment of the cables there was always enough free play to make precise throttle control at low openings almost impossible. Add to this the slack in the drive train (caused by the cushioning springs in the clutch hub which lessens shock to transmission gears and the rubber blocks in the rear wheel hub between it and the rear sprocket) and the ride was jerky unless great care was used when opening and closing the throttle.

The overall finish of the TX500 is absolutely first-rate. Chromium plated fenders, exhaust pipes and mufflers, wheel rims and handlebars are set off by beautifully applied paint (bronze, gold and black in this case) with no runs or imperfections anywhere. The fiberglass side covers are easily detachable to give access to the bulk of the electrical wiring and tool kit, and the battery is easily serviced by raising the seat.

Electrical components are also without fault. Most of the wiring is concealed to protect it from damage, and the lights are more than adequate for traveling at legal speeds at night. The only complaint we had was the horn. At 60 mph, blowing the horn could hardly be heard by the rider, much less by a person in an automobile or a pedestrian.

Many nice touches are evident, like the allen head screws which replace the phillips head screws on the engine sidecovers and rocker box assembly. An oil filter canister which removes impurities from the engine/transmission oil is located behind the countershaft sprocket cover and just below the countershaft sprocket. The air cleaner element is quite large and is easy to remove for cleaning or replacement by lifting up the seat and removing a snap-on cover.

Generally speaking, the Yamaha TX500 is a notable newcomer to this displacement category, both in its degree of refinement and execution. Generalities aside, it's a machine a lot of people have been waiting for for a long time—a 500 Twin in classic configuration, incorporating the latest technical advances of the '70s.

Two of the TX500's internal chains are shown here. The longer one runs from the starter motor and the one behind drives the Omni-phase balancer.

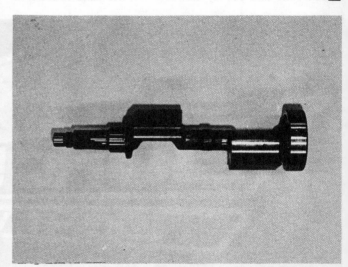

The Omni-phase balancer is chain-driven from the crankshaft with its weight 180 degrees out of phase with the crankshaft weights.

Twin overhead camshafts are driven by a duplex chain. One cam lobe opens each pair of valves.

Twin Keihin CV carburetors supply the engine with fuel. This is Yamaha's first use of the Keihin carburetor.

YAMAHA TX500

SPECIFICATIONS

List price	$1350
Suspension, front	telescopic fork
Suspension, rear	swinging arm
Tire, front	3.25-19
Tire, rear	4.00-18
Brake, front, effective diameter x width, in.	(2) 11.25 x 1.46
Brake, rear, diameter x width, in.	7.1 x 1.2
Total brake swept area, sq. in.	117
Brake loading, lb./sq. in. (160-lb. rider)	5.1
Engine, type	dohc vertical Twin
Bore x stroke, in., mm	2.87 x 2.35, 73 x 59.6
Piston displacement, cu. in., cc	30.5, 498
Compression ratio	9.0:1
Claimed bhp @ rpm	48 @ 8500
Claimed torque @ rpm, lb.-ft.	32.6 @ 6500
Carburetion	(2) Keihin CV32
Ignition	battery and coil
Oil system	gear pump, wet sump
Oil capacity, pt.	6
Fuel capacity, U.S. gal.	3.4
Recommended fuel	premium
Starting system	electric; kick, folding crank
Lighting system	12V alternator
Air filtration	dry treated paper
Clutch	multi-plate, wet
Primary drive	gear
Final drive	single-row chain
Gear ratios, overall:1	
5th	6.16
4th	7.37
3rd	8.83
2nd	11.83
1st	17.82
Wheelbase, in.	55.8
Seat height, in.	32.0
Seat width, in.	10.0
Handlebar width, in.	30.0
Footpeg height, in.	12.4
Ground clearance, in.	7.0 (at stand)
Curb weight (w/half-tank fuel), lb.	433
Weight bias, front/rear, percent	47/53
Test weight (fuel and rider), lb.	593
Mileage at completion of test	2520

TEST CONDITIONS

Air temperature, degrees F	86
Humidity, percent	36
Barometric pressure, in. hg.	29.92
Altitude above mean sea level, ft.	383
Wind velocity, mph	5-7
Strip alignment, relative wind:	

PERFORMANCE

Top speed (actual @ 7910 rpm), mph	98
Computed top speed in gears (@9000 rpm), mph:	
5th	112
4th	94
3rd	78
2nd	61
1st	39
Mph/1000 rpm, top gear	12.45
Engine revolutions/mile, top gear	4815
Piston speed (@ 9000 rpm), ft./min.	3525
Lb./hp (160-lb. rider)	12.4
Fuel consumption, mpg	47
Speedometer error:	
50 mph indicated, actually	46
60 mph indicated, actually	57
70 mph indicated, actually	65
Braking distance:	
from 30 mph, ft.	29
from 60 mph, ft.	106
Acceleration, zero to:	
30 mph, sec.	2.8
40 mph, sec.	3.9
50 mph, sec.	4.6
60 mph, sec.	5.4
70 mph, sec.	7.1
80 mph, sec.	10.2
90 mph, sec.	16.2
Standing one-eighth mile, sec.	8.79
terminal speed, mph	76.59
Standing one-quarter mile, sec.	14.32
terminal speed, mph	87.12

ACCELERATION / ENGINE AND ROAD SPEEDS / RPM X 100

■ TO ADULTS, the term superbike is reserved for a rather unique 750cc or larger machine with two things going for it: unbelievable performance and styling to match. To teenagers just getting into motorcycling, though, bikes like this are no more than dreams— dreams which may become reality some day, but dreams nonetheless.

Still, for the pre-teen or teenager, reality does exist in the motorcycle world. There are even superbikes. Industry calls these mini-cycles, and in this field Yamaha was first with its off-road Mini Enduro.

For '73, Yamaha has improved the enduro and has introduced a mini-roadster called the RD60 for those with a touch of Ago in their blood. Because it's the newer model of the two, let's consider the RD60 first.

As far as styling goes, RD could very well stand for "racing department." The gas tank is very long, slim, and blends gracefully into a short but amply padded seat. The seat is curved up at the rear and has an end section, similar to those fitted to racing machines. A regular fender, however, protrudes beyond this and forms a mounting area for the taillight and turn signal assemblies.

Up front, there is a low mounted chrome front fender, a generously sized headlight, a speedometer and even a tachometer. The tach, incidentally, is red lined at 10,000 rpm and if you persist, the little Single will just touch that figure in the lower gears.

Thoughts of turning 10,000 revs and that styling kind of makes you wonder whether or not the bike is a noisy, tempermental bullet. Happily, this is not the case. The 60cc, 4.9-bhp Single starts on the first or second kick every time and at idle, it can hardly be heard at all.

Ease the machine into gear, it's a five-speed with a standard down for low shift pattern, and begin to let out the clutch. There isn't much power down low so you either have to ride the clutch or put up with a sluggish start until the tach needle nears the 6000 rpm mark. Here the engine begins to pull strongly and continues to do so right up to indicated red line.

The rpm must be kept up, but it isn't objectionable on the RD. In fact, if the tach were disconnected, you'd never believe the crank was turning that fast. There just isn't any vibration, intake roar, or exhaust noise, to indicate the rpm. Yamaha has really done its homework in this area.

YAMAHA STREET AND TRAIL MINIS

The Ever Popular Mini Enduro
Gets A New Riding Partner

Gear selection is precise and this aids acceleration considerably. If you really get with it, 23-sec. quarter mile times in the 52 mph bracket are possible and that, friends, is just about as fast as a 40-bhp VW.

Armed with this knowledge, and keeping in mind the fact that a VW has a lot more top end acceleration and speed than an RD60, we ventured out onto the boulevard. Surprisingly, the tiny Yamaha keeps up with city traffic quite nicely and is actually a delight to ride around.

Handling is incredible. Steering is so light it feels as though it is power assisted and the bike can be flicked through a series of bends with ease. Decreasing radius turns are particularly delightful because you can lean the RD over at crazy angles and still nothing drags.

On rough streets, the ride isn't particularly harsh, but you do run into the definite pogo effect found on a lot of small bikes. The cause is inadequate damping in the rear suspension components, and the only cure is substitution of better spring damper assemblies. If you go this route, however, make sure the spring rate is the same as stock.

Unlike the rear, front suspension is superb. Front forks are oil dampened internal spring units with rubber boots to keep road dirt and water out of the oil seals. They are perfectly capable of handling any common road irregularity and only bottom occassionally in chuck holes with a 160-lb. rider on board.

With its 17-in. wheels, double cradle frame, and willing engine, the RD is right on in every respect but one: brakes.

The brakes are single leading shoe both front and rear and quite frankly, are not capable of halting the bike repeatedly from top speed (52.91 mph) without considerable fade. Also, the front brake feels spongy, indicating that the outer housing on the cable is compressing slightly when the lever is withdrawn. Fortunately, around town at slower speeds, the problem does not arise. It's just that we like to have a greater margin of safety than the RD60 units provide.

So much for potential Agostinis. Take a turn off-road and enter the realm of the 80cc GT1, Yamaha's updated Mini Enduro.

The Mini Enduro first appeared in 1971, in 60cc configuration. That original was also for off-road only. Add a larger 80cc two-stroke Single and full street legal equipment and you end up with Yamaha's current offering.

As we've just indicated, the basic package and concept is unchanged. In fact many of the components on the 80 are interchangeable with those fitted to the original. Wheels are

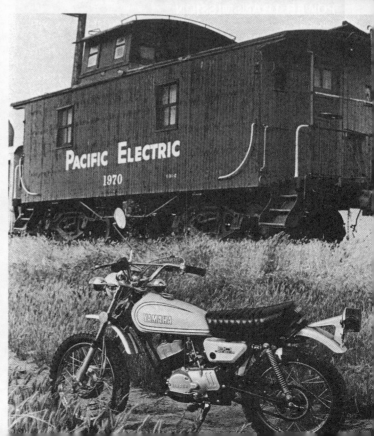

still 15 in. in front, 14 in. in the rear with 2.50 and 2.75-in. cross section tires fitted respectively. The frame is still a tiny double cradle unit with a skid plate welded in place beneath the engine. And, fenders and gas tank still have the same flare.

Forks on the new model appear different, but this is because the newer units have polished sliders whereas the originals were painted the same color as the gas tank. These forks are adequate, but are not as good as those found on several other minis. Most forks are like those found on the RD60 with springs and damping units in each leg. Not so on

the GT1. Here we find a spring in one leg and an oil damper assembly in the other. Bolt the front wheel in place and you have a front end that behaves in a normal manner—only not quite as well as a conventional setup.

Hit a washboard road on the GT1 and the forks top and bottom a lot. Also the front end skates around because inadequate rebound damping lets the front wheel bounce more than conventional forks.

The rear suspension components could stand some improvement as well. As with the RD60, spring rate is fine, but damping is totally lacking.

As mentioned earlier, the GT1 is powered by an 80 instead of 60cc two-stroke Single. Instead of using a rotary valve setup with the carburetor hidden in the engine case, the new engine features a reed valve arrangement with a conventionally mounted carburetor. Surprisingly, the 80 only puts out 0.4 bhp more and is still rated at less than 5 bhp. Apparently the changeover was more in the interest of increased torque and reliability than anything else.

Since the unit is of similar design to the RD60, we suspected a five-speed transmission. Such, however, is not the

YAMAHA RD60

SPECIFICATIONS

List price	$359
Suspension, front	telescopic fork
Suspension, rear	swinging arm
Tire, front	2.50-17
Tire, rear	2.50-17
Engine, type	two-stroke Single
Bore x stroke, in., mm	1.65 x 1.56, 42.0 x 39.7
Piston displacement, cu. in., cc	3.36, 55
Compression ratio	6.9:1 (corrected)
Claimed bhp @ rpm	4.9 @ 8000
Claimed torque @ rpm lb.-ft.	3.4 @ 6500
Piston speed @ rpm ft./min.	2080 @ 8000
Carburetion	VM 16 SH Mikuni
Ignition	flywheel magneto
Oil system	oil injection
Oil capacity, pt.	2.2
Fuel capacity, U.S. gal.	2.1
Recommended fuel	premium
Starting system	kick, folding crank
Air filtration	oil-wetted foam

POWER TRANSMISSION

Clutch	multi-plate, wet
Primary drive	gear
Final drive	single-row chain
Gear ratios, overall:1	
5th	12.03
4th	14.09
3rd	17.88
2nd	25.05
1st	40.70

DIMENSIONS

Wheelbase, in.	47
Seat height, in.	28.5
Seat width, in.	8.5
Handlebar width, in.	23.5
Footpeg height, in.	10.0
Ground clearance, in.	6.5
Curb weight (w/half-tank fuel), lb.	164
Weight bias, front/rear, percent	44.5/55.5

PERFORMANCE

Top speed (actual @ 9780 rpm, mph	52.91
Standing one-eighth mile, sec.	16.49
terminal speed, mph	48.41
Standing one-quarter mile, sec.	23.30
terminal speed, mph	52.53

case. The GT1 still has a four-speed unit with neutral at the top of the shift pattern. Although gear selection is positive, we would prefer a transmission with neutral located between first and second and low gear at the bottom of the pattern. Since the GT1 does not shift conventionally, it is not as good a training device for the novice rider.

By today's standards, the GT1 lacks a certain amount of sophistication, especially in the area of suspension. But one thing is undeniable. The bike is an absolute ball to ride. You can pull second gear wheelies on straights, slam on the brakes (they work fine on this one) and dive into a corner in true class C fashion. On slippery surfaces, the front end will push a little, but it's not alarming and the rear end rarely breaks loose. When the rear does break loose, the entire machine will drift to the outside, slowing as it drifts. Spills should be rare.

Like most small bikes, however, the GT1 is not a jack of all trades. When negotiating soft ground the front end plows and there is barely enough power to keep the bike going. Likewise, caution is advised on streets (the GT1 does come with full legal equipment). The machine is very small, will be difficult to see and will just barely exceed 45 mph. This is fine for mounting roads or for riding within national parks, but for little else.

There you have it, Yamaha's minis for street and trail. The GT1 offers a lot of fun for the money and the RD60, well, it's got to be one of the cheapest ways to get around town! ◙

YAMAHA 80GT1

SPECIFICATIONS

List price	$356
Suspension, front	telescopic fork
Suspension, rear	swinging arm
Tire, front	2.50-15
Tire, rear	2.75-14
Engine, type	two-stroke Single
Bore x stroke, in., mm	1.85 x 1.65, 47 x 42
Piston displacement, cu. in., cc	4.39, 72
Compression ratio	6.8:1 (corrected)
Claimed bhp @ rpm	4.9 @ 6500
Claimed torque @ rpm lb.-ft.	4.0 @ 6000
Piston speed @ rpm ft./min.	1787 @ 6500
Carburetion	16mm Teikei
Ignition	flywheel magneto
Oil system	oil injection
Oil capacity, pt.	1.5
Fuel capacity, U.S. gal.	1.3
Recommended fuel	premium
Starting system	kick, folding crank
Air filtration	oil-wetted foam

POWER TRANSMISSION

Clutch	multi-plate, wet
Primary drive	gear
Final drive	single-row chain
Gear ratios, overall:1	
5th	none
4th	11.79
3rd	14.97
2nd	20.96
1st	34.06

DIMENSIONS

Wheelbase, in.	42.0
Seat height, in.	26.0
Seat width, in.	9.0
Handlebar width, in.	25.0
Footpeg height, in.	9.5
Ground clearance, in.	7.0
Curb weight (w/half-tank fuel), lb.	140
Weight bias, front/rear, percent	46/54

PERFORMANCE

Top speed (actual @ 9520 rpm, mph	46.85
Standing one-eighth mile, sec.	16.78
terminal speed, mph	43.90
Standing one-quarter mile, sec.	24.40
terminal speed, mph	46.70

YAMAHA'S ALMOST complete domination of Class C 250 road racing and Novice flat track events is legendary. The lightweight TD, and now the waterpumper version of the Yamaha 250 Twin, has been nearly invincible in all forms of competition in which it is entered.

As you'd expect, it's pretty difficult (and costly) to get hold of one of these racers but Yamaha has nearly always made a purely street version available to the general public...a street version which incorporates many of the features designed specifically for competition. The RD250A is no exception and shows its racing heritage strongly in several important areas: styling, design, performance, and handling qualities.

Styling wise, the machine is slim, lean, and businesslike, at least as far as Japanese machines go. There is almost an absence of useless chromed frills to dazzle prospective customers. Instead, we find a clean gas tank, much like the one fitted on earlier Triumph Trophy models, which blends in nicely with a long black saddle, black engine package and conservatively contoured chromed fenders.

The RD250A engine is significantly different in appearance from the earlier YDS-3 Yamahas, and is quite different on the inside, too. The horizontally split crankcase assembly has been slimmed down significantly, the bore/stroke ratio is now "square" instead of "oversquare" (bigger bore than stroke), and there is a sixth speed in the transmission. The crankcase, cylinders and cylinder heads are now finished in a matte black paint, with polished fin edges and raised, polished lettering and accent strips on the crankcase edges. It is truly a handsome package, and one which is quite a bit smaller in bulk than the earlier Twins.

Oil for the transmission and the clutch is contained within the crankcase and oil for engine lubrication is delivered from a separate oil tank through the intake manifolds via a plunger pump whose delivery is dependent on the throttle opening and engine rpm. This oil mixes with the incoming fuel/air charge and is circulated through the engine, lubricating the connecting rods, pistons and central main bearings.

The biggest difference from earlier Yamaha two-stroke Twins is the incorporation of a reed valve induction system. In this system, there are seven ports in the cylinders which control the circulation of the incoming fuel/air charge after it has passed through the reed valve. But the inlet charge is controlled by the reed valve rather than the mechanical opening and closing of the inlet port by the piston's moving up and down, or by the opening and closing of a rotary valve. Therefore, even if you turn the throttle open wide at low rpm, the engine will accept no more fuel/air mixture than it can use through the reed valve.

The 7th port is actually an extension of the inlet port and extends upward into the cylinder. This "port" improves performance by allowing more fuel/air mixture to be "rammed" into the combustion chamber and by simultaneously improving the removal of burned exhaust gases. This system yields smooth throttle response and aided in our obtaining a 58 mpg fuel consumption figure during ordinary street and highway riding. The fuel economy is fantastic; but there is one problem. Visible smoke. Our test RD smoked enough to make us self-conscious. Leaning the mixture out slightly would help, but more needs to be done than rejetting to cure the problem.

The crankshaft assembly rides on four main bearings so it won't flex under high rpm loadings, and the clutch is driven from the crankshaft by a helical cut gear for mechanical silence. Clutch lever pressure is remarkably low and no slippage was noted, even after a hard day at the drag strip. An adequate clutch is particularly important on a 250 roadster as starting off when packing double requires "riding" the clutch in order to keep the engine from balking.

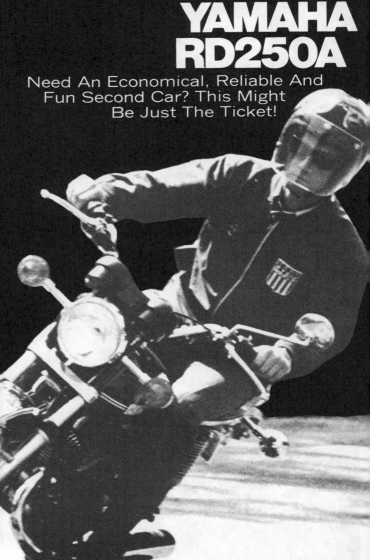

YAMAHA RD250A

Need An Economical, Reliable And Fun Second Car? This Might Be Just The Ticket!

Still, the clutch had an annoying characteristic. It was a little "chattery" when taking up the drive. This characteristic is often present in new machines, and more often then not it disappears as the clutch beds in. Our machine was getting smoother, but it was still a little jerky in taking up the drive, right up until the end of the test.

In typically Japanese fashion, the transmission mainshaft and layshaft are located one behind the other in a horizontal plane. The shifting drum and four girdling-type shifter forks are located below the transmission shafts. This shifting setup is employed on almost all motorcycles produced today, and works extremely well on the Yamaha. The gear ratios are necessarily spaced rather close together because of the power characteristics of the engine, but shifting is a delight. Moving from gear to gear requires minimal effort and gear lever travel is short.

Just sitting on the firm seat and grasping the narrow handlebars indicates that the RD250A was intended for some aggressive riding. One ride on a race track confirms it. Yamaha has a handler in the RD250. Really, it's a bike that begs to be pushed to the limit!

Fine handling qualities in this case can be attributed directly to the frame. Patterned closely after the highly successful Yamaha competition machines, the frame is a double downtube, single toptube design with a seat rail connecting up forward to the downtubes just below the steering head and extending rearward to provide a mounting platform for the seat and attachment point for the rear fender. Fabricated from mild steel, the frame is very sturdy in appearance and in fact. Flexing does not occur. Welding is a little crude in appearance, but penetration appears to be good.

Braking is another area in which the RD250A scores highly. Using drum brakes on both wheels, the bike has a brake swept area of 61 sq. in., which gives a brake loading of slightly over 8 lb./sq. in. with a 160-lb. rider on board. Try as we might, we couldn't get the brakes hot enough to fade severely, not even

after several miles of downhill braking in the mountains. Brake pedal and lever pressures are only moderate, and braking "feel" is certainly above average.

Electrically, the Yamaha is above average, as well. Wiring is the plug-in type and almost all the electrical components are accessible for servicing by removing the alternator cover and raising the seat. The exception is the high tension coils which are located under the gasoline tank, but they rarely need attention, anyway. Lighting is on a par with other Japanese machines. The dimmer switch, horn button and flasher switches are located on the left handgrip and the lighting switch and an off-run-off switch nestle on the right handgrip. A nicely laid out instrument panel contains the speedometer and tachometer, turn indicator lamps, a headlight high beam indicator and a red light which tells the rider when the brake light is working. The neutral indicator lamp is inside the tachometer face, but it is obscured by the front brake cable.

The speedometer and tachometer are both large and easy to see, but sunlight reflecting off the faces makes them difficult to read at times. A non-glare glass for the lenses would be a>

nice touch. Also, the rear brake indicator light and the high beam indicator light are distracting when riding at night. We feel they could be toned down quite a bit and still be visible during daylight.

The underseat area is nicely laid out to facilitate servicing items located under it. At the front, near the gasoline tank, is an area for the toolkit. The kit contains all tools needed to perform routine service, but is only of mediocre quality. Under the space for the toolkit is the top of the air cleaner box, which is held on by a rubber strap that can be removed in seconds for cleaning or changing the air filter element. Just behind the air cleaner is the battery with its cell tops readily accessible for easy checking of the electrolyte level. And behind the battery is the oil tank filler cap. The seat, incidentally, locks, but not automatically, so the rider has a choice.

Riding the RD250A is a thrill. Starting from cold requires the use of the choke for a period of a minute or so to get the engine running smoothly. And then for the first few blocks, the engine is reluctant to accept large throttle openings. This hesitation disappears completely when the Twin reaches

YAMAHA

operating temperature. Shifting the six-speed transmission is one of the nicest feelings a motorcyclist can experience. Practically no lever pressure is necessary to snick the transmission from one ratio to the next, and all the other controls work so well that we couldn't fault them.

But the RD250A is designed as a sports and commuting machine rather than a long distance tourer. The narrow seat is very firm and becomes uncomfortable after long periods in the saddle. The suspension is also a little too firm for long distance riding. Where the RD250 really shines is flicking it through corners on a winding, mountain road or it's a good machine for small-bore production racing. There is very little engine power below 4000 rpm or so, and using the transmission is a necessity to keep the engine revs up in the power band.

The RD250A is extremely well balanced and leans readily in either direction. The side and center stands are easily accessible to the rider, but are tucked up out of the way so that they don't drag when cornering. Nice! Charging through alternating right and left handers is easier than on any other 250 we've tested. Very little body english is required. Just pitch it in and gas it. Speaking of gassing it, the RD also pulls neat 2nd gear wheelies!

The seat-handlebar-footpeg relationship is very good for riders under 5 ft., 11 in., but even with one person on board the seat strap for the rear passenger gets in the way. Unless the rider is short, carrying a passenger over long distances will be uncomfortable.

As indicated earlier, the suspension is a little on the stiff side, but this permits the rider to negotiate high speed corners without the machine weaving or bottoming out over bumps. Like we said, the RD250A is a sporting machine with almost all the attributes one could ask for. But a long distance tourer it is not. For it's intended purpose we find it difficult to fault. It's one of the best, but its larger brother, the RD350, is an interesting piece of equipment, too, and only costs a few dollars more.... ◙

Warranty	6 mo./4000 mi.
Major Tuneup (inc. oil change, etc.)	$22.50
Air Filter Element	$4.32
Rear Tire (standard)	$19.95
Drive Chain (standard)	$37.86
Sealed Beam	$7.20
Taillight Bulb	76 cents
Turn Indicator Bulbs	70 cents
Battery	$10.62
Ignition Parts:	
Points	(2) @ $4.94
Condenser	(2) @ $1.68
High Tension Coil	(2) @ $8.54

YAMAHA RD250A

SPECIFICATIONS

List price	$719
Suspension, front	telescopic fork
Suspension, rear	swinging arm
Tire, front	3.00-18
Tire, rear	3.25-18
Brake, front, diameter x width, in.	7.09 x 1.38
Brake, rear, diameter x width, in.	7.09 x 1.38
Total brake swept area, sq. in.	61
Brake loading, lb./sq. in. (160-lb. rider)	8.16
Engine, type	two-stroke Twin
Bore x stroke, in., mm	2.13 x 2.13, 54 x 54
Piston displacement, cu. in., cc	15.07, 247
Compression ratio	6.7:1 (corrected)
Claimed bhp @ rpm	N.A.
Claimed torque @ rpm, lb.-ft.	N.A.
Carburetion	(2) Mikuni VM 28 SC
Ignition	coil and battery
Oil system	oil injection
Oil capacity, pt.	4.2
Fuel capacity, U.S. gal.	3.2
Recommended fuel	premium
Starting system	kick, folding crank
Lighting system	12V alternator
Air filtration	dry treated paper
Clutch	multi-plate, wet
Primary drive	helical gear
Final drive	single-row chain
Gear ratios, overall:1	
6th	6.80
5th	7.67
4th	8.96
3rd	11.38
2nd	15.34
1st	22.15
Wheelbase, in.	52.8
Seat height, in.	31.1
Seat width, in.	10.0
Handlebar width, in.	29.5
Footpeg height, in.	11.7
Ground clearance, in.	6.5
Curb weight (w/half-tank fuel), lb.	333
Weight bias, front/rear, percent	44/56
Test weight (fuel and rider), lb.	468
Mileage at completion of test	409

TEST CONDITIONS

Air temperature, degrees F	73
Humidity, percent	65
Barometric pressure, in. hg.	29.97
Altitude above mean sea level, ft.	468
Wind velocity, mph	0-2
Strip alignment, relative wind:	

PERFORMANCE

Top speed (actual @8300 rpm), mph	89
Computed top speed in gears (@8500 rpm), mph:	
6th	91
5th	80
4th	69
3rd	54
2nd	40
1st	28
Mph/1000 rpm, top gear	10.7
Engine revolutions/mile, top gear	5630
Piston speed (@8500 rpm), ft./min.	3018
Lb./hp (160-lb. rider)	N.A.
Fuel consumption, mpg	58
Speedometer error:	
50 mph indicated, actually	45
60 mph indicated, actually	54
70 mph indicated, actually	62
Braking distance:	
from 30 mph, ft.	37
from 60 mph, ft.	134
Acceleration, zero to:	
30 mph, sec.	3.1
40 mph, sec.	4.0
50 mph, sec.	5.2
60 mph, sec.	7.4
70 mph, sec.	10.5
80 mph, sec.	15.0
Standing one-eighth mile, sec.	9.37
terminal speed, mph	69.60
Standing one-quarter mile, sec.	15.64
terminal speed, mph	80.71

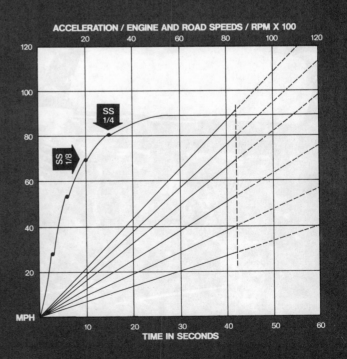

ACCELERATION / ENGINE AND ROAD SPEEDS / RPM X 100

start wind

Yamaha TA-125 Road Racer

With One Of These Screamers And $1647, You Too Can Be a Boy Racer ...For At Least A Year / By John Waaser

YEARS AGO, the Norton Manx was "King of the Isle," and Matchbox was more than just a line of toy cars. Matchless, Norton's poor stepbrother in the AMC combine, produced a road racer similar to the Manx, but a bit less sophisticated.

Known as the G-50, in typical Matchless letter-number fashion, the bike was furnished in a slightly lower state of tune than the Manx, and used a single, chain-driven overhead camshaft, rather than the Manx's tower-shaft-driven double knocker setup.

The Matchless G-50 was preceded by the AJS 7R, from which the G-50 was developed. The 7R was produced in 1947 as a racer which would be easy and cheap for the average rider to maintain. With a displacement of only 350cc, it was slightly slower than either of the 500s; just right for the fainthearted road racer who couldn't feature zipping down Bray Hill at a buck fifty or so. It also cost quite a bit less, and it

proved to be less dear to maintain through a season of racing. Officially designated the 7R, it quickly earned an affectionate nickname—"The Boy Racer."

Yamaha in recent years has become the undisputed leader of the 250cc class in American road racing, and hasn't done too badly in the open class, either, in spite of a large displacement handicap. And now, quietly, Yamaha has introduced a new Boy Racer—a bike which sells for less than a grand (to the dealer), can be raced most economically throughout the season, and which is fully capable of doing in even much larger competitive mounts. At the Pocono road race this year, for instance, young Dana Dandeneau hopped on his TA-125 in his first AMA road race and walked away from the pack. And that

was a combined race of up to 200cc bikes.

Bob Fairbairn works for Boston Cycles; he confiscated one of the first examples of the breed to come into that area, and proceeded to race it in AAMRR (the eastern Alphabet Club) events.

Bob also is a road racing freak. So is his boss; so, it was arranged that Bob would have a day off to take the bike and this nervous novice up to Bryar Motorsport Park for a day of play on the machine.

We arrived at Bryar with half of Boston Cycles service department, the TA-125, a 350 waterpumper, a 350cc Kawasaki cafe racer Triple and a 750cc BMW. The 125 looked like a boy's motorcycle in that company, and out on the track it was the only one of the

four which wailed. I mean there was no doubt just which bike was headed your way, even with earplugs.

After Bob warmed the 125 up, I was encased in protective leathers and loaned a Bell Star, in preference to my shieldless Magnum. The bike was ready, and I thought I was; after all, do I not have Tomaselli clip-ons on my street bike?

I snicked the boy racer in gear, and released the clutch. So far, so good. As I got moving, I picked up my foot, and attempted to place it on the peg. I couldn't. Me, 5 ft. 4 in., and short-legged at that, who fits so well on the 250 Yammie; no way would my leg come up into what Bob described as the "semi-fetal position" necessary to ride this little tiddler. I stopped and tried again, this time using my right foot to prop the bike up while stopped. It

worked; a second later we were touring the course.

The pavement is deteriorating badly of late, and cars had laid a cover of oil and rubber on top, which didn't help traction. I decided that discretion was the better part of valor, and took a half-dozen easy laps before coming in to see if the controls could be arranged to better fit my bod. I was having a great deal of difficulty getting my feet on top>

Road Racer

of the shift and brake levers.

Riding a bike with a 13,000 rpm red line doesn't upset me much; my street bike has a five-figure red line. But the narrow powerband, coupled with an uncommon willingness to exceed the red line, keeps you busy until you get used to the feel of the engine and know where to shift pulling into and out of each corner. What will really set you free, however, is riding a bike which will bog, and almost die, when you crank the throttle on at eight grand in second gear. Now that's a completely foreign experience to most of us!

The shift pattern is Early Japanese Reversed—that is, one up, and four down, on the left. The reverse is due to the linkage.

The controls were adjusted to their limits already, and Bob says the only thing to do was get used to them. From

my experience with fitting clip-ons to my street bike, I know that the body can make these adjustments in time, but it was becoming more obvious that this bike was a "boy racer" in a much more literal sense than was the 7R.

Other than the controls, the bike felt delightful. Handling is quick; but the bike still felt stable at the speeds I was going (over 100 on the straights, very slowly in the turns), and the brakes were superb. The engine was smooth, and, as long as you kept it in the power band (10,500 to 12,500 rpm) it was most impressive for a 125.

From Loudon, it was out to lunch, then back to Boston Cycles for a minor teardown, and a look at what it costs to go racing. Yamaha brought about 400 of these modern-day boy racers into the states this year. It is obvious from the price that the bike must be derived

essentially from stock components—and a quick look will confirm that the frame and engine appear to be stock 100cc LS-2 street bike parts—the frame even has the center stand lugs still on it.

Even things which are different are the same; the brakes, obviously, are not LS-2 items—but they do look familiar. They're lifted straight off Yamaha's 200cc road burner, with racing linings installed. Light in weight, and powerful enough for the machine's weight and speed potential, they worked superbly on the track. The swinging arm is also from the 200cc machine, for a little more rigidity out back.

If you look really carefully, though, you can see a small difference in the frame. The top rear frame tubes on the LS-2 form the subframe only; they don't run up to the steering head. Those on the road racer run up to the steering head for more rigidity. The engine's bottom end is so close to stock LS-2 that it takes a parts manual to show the differences. One gear ratio is different, and a racing crank is used, with two more rollers, and racing rods which have bigger slits for oiling, silver bearing cages, and more side clearance. Even the cases are stock, and autolube is included.

The top end is strictly racing, with single-ring pistons, chrome-plated bores, trick porting, and racing carburetors. The ignition coils and "black box" are the same as on the 250cc and 350cc road racers, but the donor is a special double lead type, said to give off fewer stray sparks at the higher rpm this engine thrives on. The new 700cc Four will require a double lead donor, and Bob thinks the hot setup might be to use it on the medium-weight bikes, also. The ignition has proven quite reliable.

Other changes are the obvious ones—tank, seat, fairing, tachometer, rims and tires. The package is good for almost 50 mph in top speed over the LS-2, which will run about 73, flat out.

Use of so many stock parts creates some hassles, though. The engine design is not as modern as the larger bikes; the cases split vertically. You must have the proper tools for changing the crank, otherwise it will never go in straight. At the speeds this engine turns, out-of-round tolerances on the crank become important. Another stock part ill-suited to racing use is the wet clutch. Wet clutches tend to stick together at high rpm, and might just refuse to free immediately in the event of an impending seizure. When you hear that tell-tale tinkle from the engine, you hope your reactions are fast enough—and for sure you don't want the clutch hanging up.

But it is amazing just how good a

Note bottom end of support struts.

Stock piston is on right. Modified piston has oil grooves, skirt is cut, transfer area shaped.

Road Racer

racing bike Yamaha has been able to develop using stock off-the-shelf parts. And nobody can deny the cost advantages of this system. With this machine, a youngster can get started in road racing for about the same money as a competitive motocrosser, and maintenance for the year shouldn't be any higher, either. Initial cost varies according to the dealer. If a rider is good enough, or the dealer anxious enough, you might get the bike at cost. If not, most dealers charge from $1200 to $1500 for the bike, without a fairing. The fairing is $105, dealer cost. Japanese racing tires are fondly referred to as rim protectors. They will have to be replaced for any serious racing, with Dunlops; dealer cost is about $40 there.

If you're really starting from scratch, figure $200 or so for leathers, boots and helmet, and you may need a trailer, if you have no other way to transport the bike. At most, if you buy everything in the same place, it should cost you $2000, starting from ground zero. Dealer cost on even the air-cooled 250cc road racer alone is well above that figure, so the TA-125 offers cheap racing indeed.

You'll have to do a minor top end job between each race. This will involve two rings, at $4.15 each, wrist pin bearings (same as the street bike) at $2 each, two wrist pins at 65 cents, four clips at 10 cents each, two base gaskets at 15 cents, and two head gaskets at 35 cents each. You'll also want to change the transmission oil between races; oil is cheap, so buy the best SAE 30 automotive oil you can. Every second race, figure on replacing the pistons, too, at $11 each. All these prices are retail.

If you should be unfortunate enough to score a barrel, it will zing you $60, but you have to be pretty ham-fisted to do that, says Bob. The crank is good for about eight races, and costs the dealer $47. On parts like this, the markup can be high—as much as double the cost plus 10 percent. Clutch plates should be replaced with the crank. If you have the facilities, you can rebuild the crank and save a few bucks there. Bob has run the season on one crank, with a rebuild, and will replace it over the winter.

Bob says the tires should last all year. You might want to replace them before that, since any good tire will harden as it gets used. At any rate, tire mileage will be very much better than with the big bikes. He says the 428H chain will go all year if it is well maintained. Sprockets are steel, and since you will carry two or three of each for gearing changes, they should go the year also. Rear sprockets are $11, retail, while

countershaft sprockets are $4.50. Stock shock absorbers are not so great, and a new set on Bob's bike lost their damping in three races. They retail for $80 a pair.

A careful accounting of expenses for the year for Bob came to $1647 and change, at net prices, excluding such things as spark plugs and oil used at the track and not recorded. Getting a sponsorship for an unknown rider may be difficult, but many dealers are offering a contingency award program. Last year Boston Cycles awarded contingency prizes to scrambles riders, and Mark Robillard, virtually unknown at the beginning of the year, collected about $1500, at $25 per heat win, $50 per overall win, and $500 for a class championship. Such a system awards a good, new rider right away, without saddling the dealer with a dud; Boston Cycles will be extending this program to certain classes of road racing in 1974. Many other dealers can be expected to institute similar programs, which, combined with the low initial cost of this machine, and the high resale value of a well-maintained bike, could well make racing a break-even venture.

As mentioned, you'll want to remove the rim protectors from the new bike, and add a fairing. But as with any new road racer, there are things you can do inside which will help, also. Bob likes to undercut the driven gears for positive engagement inside the transmission. The rest, he says, is all careful assembly and liberal use of lock-wiring to make sure parts don't fall off. Building reliability is important to the privateer, and while the fastest bikes have been slightly modified, he recommends leaving the bike stock for the first eight races or so.

Gearing, jetting, and ignition timing are really critical on this machine, and he suggests you learn to get these spot on before doing any modification. He reports some piston holing, even in stock form, especially if the machine is lugged down to eight or nine grand. There's a lot of detonation, also, and the spark should never be advanced more than 2mm BTDC. Everything happens quickly with the little tiddlers; there isn't much warning of a seizure, and if you seize, or scrape a peg, there's no warning at all of the impending damage to your backside. "One minute you're driving along, the next minute your hands are empty," was the way he put it.

The fast guys all remove the autolube system, and run a gas/oil mix in the tank. For one thing, the rear tire tends to scrape through the oil line leading from the oil tank (in the back of the

seat) to the pump—and that is good for a certain seizure, if you don't go down first from the oil on the tire. Bob also warns about some bogus information in the manual; for instance, the book says cylinder head bolt torque should be 16 ft.-lb., when any fool knows that the bolts used won't stand more than 75 in.-lb. reliably.

The bike is a little sensitive to air gap at the CDI donor. Anything below 0.012 in., the rotor will touch the donor. So Bob uses that as a gauge. Set the gap at 12 thou, and if they touch when the crank gets to whipping at high speed (it leaves a tell-tale mark on the rotor) you know you have one race left on that crank. Lightly sand the marks off the rotor so you can tell the next time it touches. While the tach is red-lined at 13 grand, Bob says 14,000 rpm can be used if it's a question of making it into or out of the corner ahead of somebody you're dead even with. He doesn't recommend it as a constant practice, however.

Modifying the engine slightly will net an increase of one to two horsepower. Modifications include cylinder head squish area shape, cutting and shaping the bottom of the pistons, altering the ports slightly, smoothing the ports for better flow, and cutting grooves in the pistons to hold oil for better lubrication. A few racers find the brand of oil is critical, also, as some of the synthetics will drop the rpm range considerably; Bob likes Castrol "R." If all this sounds like a lot of work for a few extra horses, it is. But Bob is running a 3.00-18 KR96 rear tire; something the stock engine just will not pull. He thinks that gives him an advantage, too.

The swinging arm rubber bushings should be replaced for maximum stability. Frank Camillieri is tooling up to make a swinging arm out of 1 x 1½ in. rectangular tubing. It will have metal bushings, and will be set up to accept Koni or Girling shocks at the rear, which the stock swinging arm will not. In view of the shock problems encountered, this swinging arm should be a good investment, at about $100. Bob also is thinking about shortening the tank to move the seat forward, to help the seating position a bit, as well as put more weight on the front end. He reports the front end feels light on occasion.

The motorcycle should be exactly the same for 1974 (we rode a 1973). Bob keeps dreaming about a six-speed, water-cooled, dry clutch version which he hopes they'll introduce when the current production run is over. But then it wouldn't be a Boy Racer anymore. ◙

BOSTON CYCLES is a road-racing-oriented, multi-brand shop. But, while the woods-riding scene has risen tremendously in New England in the past few years, and Boston Cycles has sponsored some of the top motocrossers in the area, owner John Jacobson just can't get into the dirt thing.

He was a little more enthusiastic, however, when asked to merchandise some fancy gadgets made in France by Eric Sondel for the Yamaha 350. Jacobson had his mechanics set up a cafe racer for display, just to see what the response would be.

The display bike has had its up-to-date instruments replaced with older units because the crew that set it up found them more appealing aesthetically. I don't happen to agree. Besides, it would be impractical for them to do that on machines set up for resale, so they won't. Other than that, the machine would sell for $1150, new, with the parts exchanged. That is, the figure would include all of the new parts, plus the labor of installing and setting them up, but the shop would keep all parts removed in the conversion. This price is based on that of the 1974 Yamaha 350cc Twin.

The gas tank is an absolutely gorgeous formed-aluminum piece of art. But handle it with care; it scratches and dents easily. Cafe racers, it seems, are always meant to be seen and polished, but never ridden. On the plus side, it holds about 4.6 gal. of petrol, which should be good for more than 150 miles of steady cruising. That may not be much, but it's a damned sight better than any Japanese 350 will do with the stock tank.

Unfortunately, the assemblers chose to use Tommaselli clip-ons, which do not work well with this tank. The front of the tank extends into the steering head area, for "artistic" reasons only. The Tommasellis have nyloc nuts on the outside that would jam against the tank.

The immediate cure is to mount the bars farther forward than is comfortable. In this case, the left bar is even farther forward than the right one. A more long-range cure would be to modify the steering stops to give less steering lock, which is

not really all that difficult. You just drill them, and insert bolts to adjust the lock.

An even more satisfactory cure would be to specify the use of John Tickle clip-ons (made in England), which look as though they might work just fine. Dunstall clip-ons also appear to be adequate in their mounting, but they're some three inches shorter on each side, and might not accommodate the brake master cylinder on the right side, without the necessity of hanging the throttle over the edge.

The permanent solution would be to modify the tank design to allow more steering lock, especially since Tommasellis are the *ne plus ultra* of clip-ons. For now, though, I'd specify the Tickle clip-ons.

The fiberglass seat is scantily padded, but uses the stock mountings and lock, so you retain the helmet holders and the easy access to the oil tank (oil injection is also maintained), and to the battery. The toolkit resides in its conventional place, also, though you have to lift the rear of the tank a bit to get at it. These are the advantages of designing a cafe racer conversion for a particular make and model of motorcycle—particularly one as popular as the RD350/R5 series.

But what is it like to ride the beast? The R5 is already the quickest bike in its class. The Sondel conversion enhances this feeling considerably. Not that the weight reduction is that significant, it's not; but the weight transfer to the rear is indeed significant, and that makes the front end pop up even more easily than the stocker's does. It quickens the handling a whole bunch, as well.

In spite of the fact that I was told that a great deal of time and effort had gone into setting up the controls properly on this particular bike, I had the distinct impression that this was not so. It wouldn't idle properly until we fiddled with the throttle cable, for instance, and the clutch and throttle cables were very poorly routed. This is rather typical of many cafe racers, since the builder often tries to make do with the stock cables, whereas the shorter, lower bars should be fitted with somewhat shorter cables. Stock cables certainly can be used, but they must be routed so that the excess is taken up in large bends near the handlebars.

The shift linkage was stiff, but bearable; the rear brake linkage was intolerable. The rear brake pedal was hard to push, and the brake came on suddenly, without much feel, and wasn't at all powerful. You could use the front brake exclusively on this bike and never miss the rear one. The front brake, of course, was stock Yamaha, and superb, except that with the modified weight distribution, there was more than normal weight transfer.

Heavy use of the front brake made the forks wallow. This could probably be cured with either oil of higher viscosity, or with different springs and damping.

The rear brake problems could be traced to a change in leverage—since a shorter pedal is used—and to the fact that the actuating arms were not parallel—a must when setting up this type of linkage.

There were other problems, too. I had to consciously reach inward for the brake lever, and I felt that it was too narrow. But it missed the kickstart lever by only the tiniest of margins, so it obviously was designed to the limit. Cafe racers should never have kickstarters. The faint of heart should buy one with electric starting, while the staunch enthusiast should practice his run-and-bump technique.

I also got the impression that the shift lever was too wide, but that never really bothered me once under way. The shift lever barely cleared the sidestand, however, which wasn't too cool. The clutch dragged a bit, which didn't help the shifting situation; and neutral was a find-it-before-you-stop proposition.

The seat edges were hard under my thighs, especially on the right side, although it seemed that I might be able to live with that. At any rate, it should be more comfortable for a taller rider, since his thighs would be more horizontal. Raising the pegs a bit might help the shorter riders like me.

For maximum leg comfort, your thighs should be absolutely horizontal, but, of course, that increases the adjustment that the muscles in your back have to make to the lower seating position. Never fear, your muscles WILL learn to accommodate the riding position in time. The best way to help them along is to hit the throughway for about 600 miles without a rest stop. You won't be able to move for a week, even to straighten up, but after that, you will fit the bike perfectly.

Actually, the seat on this Yamaha is low enough so that the riding position is nowhere near as extreme as it looks, and it is quite comfortable even from your first moments in the saddle.

I rode the bike through the heart of Boston—hardly its element. The shift and brake linkages, the sticky clutch, the sudden rush of power from the peppy engine, all contributed to requiring a lot of attention and to detracting from the joy of riding. If you can get into a real cut-and-thrust battle with traffic, there's no doubt that the light steering and instant wheelies could make you the scourge of the Detroit Tank crowd.

But I just wish that I could have had this bike on some of the roads near home, where I could have pretended that I was Kenny Roberts, and every car that loomed in sight was Gary Nixon. Then I would have forgotten all about the stiff linkages; and the peaky power band would have been sheer ecstasy.

The large aluminum tank, especially when only partially full, acts as a sounding board for the engine noises. In the city, that, too, was a drag. But on a winding back road, it would have contributed immeasurably to my fantasy.

If you believe that motorcycle riding should never be dull or boring, and if you have access to the sort of roads that cry

out to be ridden, this bike will give you all of the thrills that you can expect from a cafe racer. And, at half the price of most, with nearly all of the labor already done for you, it's a hell of a buy.

Better yet, if you already have a 350 Yammie, the individual parts are available. Just contact Boston Cycles. ◙

ABOVE
The formed-aluminum tank is an object d' art.

CENTER
The seat uses stock mounts, so easy access to oil tank and battery is retained. It's neat but not so comfy.

BELOW
Headlight brackets, master cylinder and sloppy cable routing.

YAMAHA RD350B

Cycle World Road Test

■ THERE ARE FEW motorcycles in existence that can boast of a racing heritage and record like the one Yamaha 350s and 250s enjoy. All over the world, the small, nimble and quick two-stroke Twins have compiled victories unmatched by any other brand. And even more important is the fact that the majority of these wins were compiled by the non-factory riders, the privateers, because Yamaha makes their racing equipment available for sale to the public. Mr. Little Guy can buy a machine virtually identical to the ones ridden by the top factory team members. A neat deal for sure.

And even neater yet is the deal the guy in the street receives. He can buy a Yamaha RD250 or 350 and ride away on a motorcycle that will carry him back and forth to work in comfort, yet has all the advantages of a machine with a strong racing background. That means when it's time to have some

fun on a twisty road or mountain pass, he doesn't need another motorcycle. This one will do just fine, thank you.

So the choice, if you're out for one of these little zoomies, is between the 250 and 350. Considering, however, the $112 difference in price, there really isn't a choice. It's very difficult to pass up the added thrust produced by the larger 350 engine, the superb front disc brake and the small incidentals that make the 350 a better motorcycle.

For some, the adage seems to be, "Why change a good thing?" and that pretty much sums up Yamaha's feelings about their popular 350. A couple of years back (when the bike had its one and only attractive paint scheme), the 350 received reed-valves and a six-speed box, not to mention that wonderful disc brake. And since then we have seen only the inclusion of simple detail changes, nothing really major at all. And because drastic renovations are a good indication that something *needed* changing, one can see that the Yamaha RD350 is fine the way it is.

So along comes another new model year...1975. Owners of RDs will not be rushing down to their local Yamaha dealer

Underneath The Business Suit, There's A Set Of Full Racing Leathers!

wondering, "What in God's name have they done to my motorcycle?" or getting queasy feelings in their gut because the salesman will not be telling them, "Oh boy, I'll say they've changed it. Had lots of problems with them old ones. Kept breaking crankshafts and things. These new jobs are completely redesigned. Nobody'll have problems now." There is none of this with the RD series Yamahas. In fact, after the CW staff went over the new machine thoroughly, the only item we were sure that was changed was the paint scheme. Yamaha had thankfully left well enough alone.

Paint, in typical Yamaha fashion, is perhaps overly bright for many, but accent bands and striping designed by Molly are a big improvement over last year's unfinished look. Styling is identical to the past year's version, functional and simple with a blend of too much chrome. Yamaha either overdoes or underdoes their styling and paint schemes. One of these days they may reach a happy medium. But at least the paint, decal and finish quality is extremely good for a mass-produced motorcycle. If you find fault with anything in this realm, it would be with the machine welds on the frame, but the only

way they could be better is if they were done by hand, so they still rank high on the quality list.

Yamaha's 350 Twin is a middleweight machine, but what you could call a *small* middleweight. Sharing most of the same components with its smaller-in-displacement-only brother, the RD250, the 350 is actually slightly *physically* smaller than most of its major and direct competition. Kawasaki's 400 Triple (once a 350), is very capable of giving the Yamaha a run for its money, in terms of both handling and performance, and will be the machine that most people draw a comparison with. The Suzuki 380 makes for better long distance cruising than the Yammie, but won't be as happy on a road full of bends. And the Honda CB360 (by far the largest seller of the group), is merely a two-wheeled Chevrolet, appealing to those who are looking for reliable, economical transportation and nothing else. The only other machine in the 350 class capable of dealing with the Yamaha under performance conditions is the Moto Morini Sport (CW Oct. '74) but finding one of those to buy and then having the money to buy it is something else again.

Noise requirements for motorcycles are getting stiffer and stiffer all the time and most these days are plenty quiet enough. There are few that would even raise the eyebrow of a geriatric librarian. Nonetheless, the two-wheeled sport gets

head spin. Likewise, too much throttle when accelerating out of a lower gear corner can do the same. But this is not going to happen to a rider with experience, or to one who coordinates throttle with brain. In the hands of the right rider, the Yamaha can run off and *hide* from the big bruisers on their 750s and 900s. Yet, it is still not picture perfect.

Frame wise, the RD's chassis is very close to those used on the small bore Yamaha road racers. It is responsive to the *nth* degree, steers precisely but on the quick side, and suspension is taut enough to match the abilities of most riders. Swinging arm flex will only bother those riding on the ragged edge of staying upright and disaster, particularly if stock tires are in place. Once again, only mean, fast corners will show suspension flaws (too soft for the quickest riders) and some minor wallow will occur. Compared to the majority of motorcycles, ground clearance on both sides of the Yamaha is more than generous; contacting the pavement with the footpegs is a good indication that the stock tires are ready to sign off anyway, so that's a good time to roll back the throttle.

Small-bore production class racing is virtually dominated by Yamaha RD350s, and many show up, number plates intact, with very few modifications. Solid testimony to the fact that the RDs are one of the top-handling, best-performing motorcycles made.

Underneath the black paint and bright polish of the engine's outer surfaces, most of what is there remains as before. Since a few problems were reported, having to do with transmission oil seeping through a keyway on the primary gear and then continuing into the right cylinder, an O-ring is now installed on the crank near the gear to curtail the seepage. That is the whole and part of mechanical changes made to the 1975 RD350 Yamaha.

Several of our "Feedback" column letters have made mention of plug fouling problems with the RD350s; many wrote in with their own solutions. Plug fouling has been non-existent with our test model and with several other

hammered at (funny how the noisiest wheeled vehicles around, large trucks, get ignored), and bikes like the RD350 suffer. Intake tract revisions have taken the sharp edge off the drag strip times of the still-rapid 350 in an effort to whack off a bit of drone when the twin 28mm Mikunis start gulping air. Most of that hurt came in '74. No further changes were made to the induction system for 1975, or else we might have seen yet another reduction in the neck snapping qualities of the 350. As it stands, Yamaha has a fairly quiet motorcycle here, and one that still performs.

As we said, the Yamaha RD is a *physically* small-sized motorcycle. The rider feels as though he is sitting well on *top* of the machine, rather than *down* in it and part of it. Something feels amiss until a ride is taken, and all of a sudden things begin to fall into place. The RD350 responds instantly, almost too quickly for those who are used to a more mundane machine, and the rider and motorcycle truly are one. The Yamaha is narrow, low and short-coupled in a way that says the rider is in control. And he is if he is prepared for a trait that a powerful, short-wheelbase, lightweight bike has: the tendency to lift the front wheel under hard acceleration.

The yo-yo who climbs on an RD350, revs the engine up and dumps the clutch, will be on his back so fast it will make his

YAMAHA RD350B

SPECIFICATIONS

List price	$1071
Suspension, front	telescopic fork
Suspension, rear	swinging arm
Tire, front	3.00-18
Tire, rear	3.50-18
Brake, front, eff. dia. x width, in.	11.7 x 1.85
Brake, rear, diameter x width, in.	7.08 x 1.37
Total brake swept area, sq. in.	145.0
Brake loading, lb./sq. in. (160-lb. rider)	3.5
Engine, type	two-stroke, piston-port Twin
Bore x stroke, in., mm	2.510 x 2.126, 64 x 54
Piston displacement, cu. in., cc	21.18, 347
Compression ratio	6.6:1
Claimed bhp @ rpm	39 @ 7500
Claimed torque @ rpm, lb.-ft.	28.0 @ 7000
Carburetion	(2) 28mm Mikuni
Ignition	battery
Oil system	oil injection
Oil tank capacity, pt.	4.2
Fuel capacity, U.S. gal.	3.2
Recommended fuel	regular (min. octane 90)
Starting system	kick, folding crank
Lighting system	12V alternator
Air filtration	dry paper
Clutch	multi-disc, wet
Primary drive	helical gear
Final drive	530 single-row chain
Gear ratios, overall: 1	
6th	6.00
5th	6.79
4th	7.95
3rd	10.08
2nd	13.59
1st	19.66
Wheelbase, in.	52.0
Seat height, in.	32.0
Seat width, in.	10.0
Handlebar width, in.	29.0
Footpeg height, in.	12.0
Ground clearance, in.	6.1
Front fork rake angle, degrees	27.7
Trail, in.	4.17
Curb weight (w/half-tank fuel), lb.	341.0
Weight bias, front/rear, percent	44.8/55.2
Test weight (fuel and rider), lb.	510
Mileage at completion of test	1295

TEST CONDITIONS

Air temperature, degrees F	80
Humidity, percent	54
Barometric pressure, in. hg.	30.00
Altitude above mean sea level, ft.	383
Wind velocity, mph	4
Strip alignment, relative wind:	

start ◁ puiʍ ⟶

PERFORMANCE

Top speed (actual @ 8000 rpm), mph	99
Computed top speed in gears (@8500 rpm), mph	
6th	105.9
5th	93.6
4th	79.9
3rd	63.1
2nd	46.8
1st	32.3
Mph/1000 rpm, top gear	12.5
Engine revolutions/mile, top gear	4828.8
Piston speed (@ 8500 rpm), ft./min.	3011
Lb./hp (160-lb. rider)	13.07
Fuel consumption, mpg	35
Speedometer error:	
50 mph indicated, actually	46
60 mph indicated, actually	54
70 mph indicated, actually	64
Braking distance:	
from 30 mph, ft.	33
from 60 mph, ft.	132
Acceleration, zero to:	
30 mph, sec.	2.9
40 mph, sec.	3.6
50 mph, sec.	4.7
60 mph, sec.	5.9
70 mph, sec.	7.1
80 mph, sec.	9.8
90 mph, sec.	14.5
Standing one-eighth mile, sec	9.09
terminal speed, mph	77.6
Standing one-quarter mile, sec	14.369
terminal speed, mph	89.10

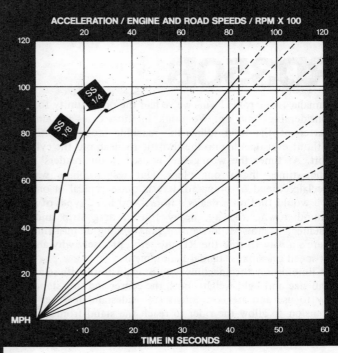

ACCELERATION / ENGINE AND ROAD SPEEDS / RPM X 100

Photography: D. Randy Riggs

PARTS PRICING

Warranty	6 mo., 4000 mi.
Major Tuneup	$37.50
Air Filter Element	$4.66
Rear Tire (standard)	$30.00
Drive Chain (standard)	$28.26
Sealed Beam	$7.20
Taillight Bulb	$.70
Turn Indicator Bulbs	$.70
Battery	$19.70
Clutch Cables	$4.10
Throttle Cables	$3.66
Brake Cables	N.A.
Ignition Parts	
Points	$4.94 ea.
Condenser	$5.10
High Tension Coil	$10.90 ea.

RD350B

Yamaha two-stroke Twins we've had the opportunity to spend considerable time on. We think in most cases it's simply a matter of the rider idling the machine around continually without ever opening up the throttle to clean out the cylinders a bit. At times the wrong fuel is used in our readers' bikes, other times the wrong plugs. Our test machine was not specially tuned or prepared; it was quite typical of one that you would find on a dealer's floor. And in all types of riding, around town, freeway, heavy traffic, drag strip and long distance, it showed no signs of plug fouling or misfiring. But there's a way to ride the RD properly, precisely why a superb six-speed gearbox is standard equipment.

Climbing on the machine you'll again notice its relatively small size and light weight. Both the center and side stands are easy to use and are convenient (the sidestand features a tab extension to allow the rider to reach the stand from a sitting position on the motorcycle), as are the remainder of the important controls. The ignition key operates the lock on the seat latch (which can be left unlocked if the rider wishes), and the fuel tank cap. The tank holds 3.2 gallons of fuel, which is good for more than 100 miles of riding before reserve is necessary. The cap deserves mention. It's of the spring-loaded flip-up variety, but it flips up *away* from the rider. Its hinge is located forward, so when the cap is up it becomes a fairly solid obstacle. Not only that, in the interest of styling, the cap is shaped attractively, unless its in the "up" position, in which case the protruding edges present knife-like jagged edges to whatever happens to contact it. In case of an accident, there remains the unlikely possibility that the cap could pop open, exposing its immobile self to an object traveling forward at great speed (i.e., the rider's body, a very vulnerable part of it). There is simply no excuse for such an oversight.

Instruments are the usual tach and speedo; a resettable trip odometer is included as well. The two dials are contained in a single housing that also positions the ignition switch directly in the center of the panel, nestled between a group of warning lights. The top two glow orange with the operation of the turn indicators, the bottom left acts as a taillight monitor and shines red whenever you touch the brakes (as long as the taillight is working). The remaining one stays red when the high beam is used. Both are far too bright; the monitor is a wasteful distraction of a gimmick, the high beam warning is so bright that the rider would almost prefer to use low beam to eliminate the red glow from his eyes. A nice soft blue (*ala* BMW) would be ample for the beam warning. The other warning we can do without completely. Another minus: the flat angle of the instrument faces reflects sunlight directly into the rider's eyes.

One almost expects an electric starter on the 350, yet there is none and one is not needed. If the engine is cold the choke lever should be depressed; once the ignition and fuel are on, all that should be needed is a few light kicks of the starter lever. The choke is required for maybe 30-45 seconds in 50-degree weather; the engine is ready to go after that.

There might be a burble or two before the engine is warmed and running crisply, but it lasts for only a minute. The six-speed transmission is the perfect mate for this humming little Twin. Pick any speed, you've got the perfect ratio for it. At 60 mph, for example, you could run in 6th at an easy pace as long as the road was level and the wind wasn't blowing strongly straight at you. Hit an incline and snick into 5th; just enough gear to keep the engine smiling. And when that guy on the 750 comes blowing past you and you feel up to playing, drop to 4th and go get him.

Braking on our test bike got better as the miles piled on. Initially there was some sponginess with the operation of the front disc, but it disappeared later in the test. This one feature gives the 350 a great advantage over the smaller RD250. The disc is large (10.5 in.) the caliper is fixed in place, and the two live pucks are each 1.75 in. in diameter, the same size as those on Yamaha's larger machines. High lever pressure is non-existent due to the use of two slave cylinders in conjunction with the master cylinder. Pressure exerted on the disc by the pucks is tremendous, without muscling effort required at the lever. Braking on the Yamaha, with a conventional but operationally good drum rear brake, is excellent.

The Yamaha should be reasonably economical to operate, needs little in the way of special tools or knowledge to maintain and provides excitement and fun on a level that few street motorcycles can match. Check the next article about our RD350 cafe racer project. It'll show you just how far you can go with the RD350. But as it stands in standard trim, surprises are in store. Underneath that business suit is a set of full racing leathers. Go ahead...the wife won't ever catch on!

By Barry Watkins

CHOOSING THE basis for a cafe bike these days can be more than a difficult choice. Sorting through the myriad accessories and equipment available for such an undertaking can be worse yet. But anyone ready to build a machine of this type *has* to make the decision, and we were no different. The choice? A Yamaha RD350 two-stroke Twin. Easy on the budget and high on performance in virtually every aspect. Now one would think that since a motorcycle is already a winner in terms of acceleration, dependability, handling and engineering, it would make it an easier job to run the full gamut. Well, yes and no. We don't have to hassle bad handling traits or bulkiness and that sort of thing. In *that* respect it's easier. But one certainly has to scratch his head and wonder what he *can* do to improve the overall machine, if cafe racing is the realm he wants to explore.

Our bike, Yamaha *de Cafito*, was designed to have the attributes of a road racer and to be totally street-legal. Many of the ideas and features incorporated can apply to other machines besides the Yamaha, so owners of other brands or models needn't stop here. Changed were the suspension, cosmetics and engine performance, keeping reliability and legality high on the list of priorities. At the same time, we wanted to reduce the overall weight somewhat.

Many cafe machines are a bit of a trade-off; some things just have to be sacrificed. Our Yamaha is no different. It won't carry two people; the riding position takes some getting used to; and the man in blue with the glowing reds is more apt to turn his eye in your direction. All the more reason for the emphasis on legality.

Yamaha RD350: A Step Further

Yamaha *de Cafito* bends in the direction of exotic from a mechanical standpoint. Many of the components you see here were designed especially for this project. The tank, seat, fender, rear-set pegs, etc. have never been seen before. Other pieces, such as the aluminum wheels, are becoming more popular with the cafe crowd as time goes on, but are still far from commonplace. How far you go is up to the size of your bank account, particularly if most of the labor is done by someone other than yourself. Keep in mind, though, that building it yourself is half the fun, as long as you know how.

By now, of course, most of our readers are aware of how cafe racing was originated in Europe. Quite simply, it was instigated by a sporting breed of rider who traversed the winding roads with his buddies; racing along from one town to another became pure sport. The guy who made it first to the next coffee or beer stop usually had the best machine or was the best rider...or both. A similar phenomenon has caught on in the U.S. of late and machines such as Yamaha *de Cafito* are being born every day. Some of the bikes are used for daily transportation and some only on a Sunday outing; many even make it into the cafe racer class at the local road race events.

Our machine began as a stocker in the showroom of Fairway Yamaha, specialists in building cafe-type machines to suit their customers' tastes. *de Cafito* started with several of Fairway's options, including clubman bars, rear-sets, seat and tank. Our major departure from the norm is probably the fact that, unlike ours, many cafe machines are big-bore models, such as the Honda 750 or Kawasaki 900. The problem with them is that they require an initial outlay of at least $1000 or more. Sometimes it's more fun to be a giant killer on a mean 350.

Frame geometry and design of the RD350 are very similar to that of the Yamaha production road racing TZ350s, much of the reason why the stockers handle so well. The advantage of going to a specialty frame would be minimal and expensive (about $500), so we shined that idea on. The stock frame would stay, though a few pieces of riffraff were removed. The next item in question was the swinging arm.

Guys who race RDs in production

class events have complained a bit about swinging arm flex, but only under pretty tough conditions. One has a good choice in this area, because there are several ways you can turn. You can get along quite well with the standard arm unless you're an exceptional rider, then you might want to try any one of the following: the standard TZ350 unit from the road racer, a Harry Hunt swinging arm, or a Don Vesco unit. To use any of these latter components, the axle holes and axle adjusters on the stock machine must be shimmed to fit. Also, the shock mounting has to be changed to a more vertical position. We decided to go ahead and try the stock unit since most of the machine's intended use would be on the street. That way it wouldn't be subjected as much to the rigors of competition.

Tank, seat and fender have their own unique style and were designed by Harold Hannemann of General Engineered Products. The tank features an aircraft type fuel filler lid that is completely flush with the top of the tank. Constructed of hand-laid fiberglass for strength, the tank is available in different lengths for different applications. The model shown holds four gallons of fuel; the stock petcock is retained. The unit was designed narrow at the front to allow ample clearance for the low bars. This way the machine can be maneuvered around as nimbly as a stocker; most cafe machines have a problem in this respect.

A new seat and tail section replace stock components and do more than look good. The seat itself is one piece, amply padded with high-quality upholstery. Utilizing stock hinges and lock latch, it can be flipped up to allow access to the storage compartment in the tail unit, a very handy touch. The

A Step Further

tail section saves a few pounds over the stock steel rear fender, especially if a smaller accessory type taillight is used in place of the bulky stocker. This particular tail section offers plenty of space to mount a license plate too. The entire tank, seat and tail section can be had for $235.

Fairings are a matter of taste, and every day there seems to be a new one on the market. Our unit comes from Dick's Cycle West (one of the major Southern California cafe racer accessory suppliers), and is called the Racer 1 3/4. It was a bear to mount—mostly because of poor brackets—and once in place shook around excessively. Since the stock headlight fits right in place in the opening provided, the shaking creates a kind of light show if you ride at night. People in front of you wonder what the heck is going on behind them with that light bobbing around. But it provides a

nice windbreak and seems to work well otherwise. Too bad it shakes. Inside our fairing we fitted a dash unit from Dick's ¼ fairing. Though trimming was necessary, it added a nice touch.

If smaller fairings are your bag, another one to consider is the ½ unit made by Cycle Craft. It includes a dash, windshield and all the necessary brackets for an easy installation. The price is about $65.

We fitted front turn signals from a Yamaha Enduro that normally mount to the handlebars. Be sure to replace the 6-volt bulbs with 12-volt items for use on the 350. Your local Sears store bicycle department sells the rear view mirrors for $3.50 each. They work pretty well too.

Bars are another preference item. Some like 'em low, some like 'em high, but the lower they are the more money you'll spend on chiropractic services. The clubman bars we used keep things to a happy medium...low wind resistance, good riding position with no need

for pain pills after a spin. J&R Manufacturing builds these out of thin-wall, heat-treated chrome moly tubing. They're strong, they're light in weight and they're comfortable. The price tag is $15.95.

Rear-set footpegs are in and work nicely in combination with a set of low bars. General Engineered Products made ours and they are designed to use the RD350's *rear* footpegs. The brackets are heat-treated aluminum, featuring flat-black paint with polished fins.

A new brake pedal and linkage set-up is employed, replacing the heavy stock pedal and yoke assembly. The brackets fit the existing holes on the muffler bracket. By using the *rear* Yamaha footpegs, the front footpeg and bar assembly (5 lb.) can be eliminated. All that one must do in the way of installation is bend the .25-inch brake rod to fit the new brake arm on the rear-set, trim off the end and fit a cotter pin. A strap included in the kit relocates the brake-light switch.

Shift linkage is simply a bolt-on operation, and total time to install rear-sets and all associated pieces is about 30 minutes. Very simple, even for the non-mechanically inclined.

WHEELS AND SUSPENSION

Forks used on the RD350 are very similar to the units fitted to larger Yamaha Enduros, with slightly different fork legs to accommodate the disc brake. Even though suspension units on a street machine don't take the rough beating that units on a motocrosser do, a few roads around can make things miserable at speed. For this reason we installed a Number One Products "Trick Kit" fork kit to give us an edge. 180ccs of 50 wt. fork oil worked well for us, as did the stock fork springs. Fork legs were turned down in a lathe for appearance and the finish is Kal-Guard's Gun Kote, with the fins polished.

We used a wide front fender for more protection from dirt and water. The unit is another product of Dick's Cycle West and weighs just 1.25 lb., trimming nearly three pounds off the total of the stock model. Aluminum brackets have to be fabricated to mount the new fender.

Even though standard 350 brakes work well, we again took things a step further. We added a disc unit at the rear (carrier, caliper and disc are standard Yamaha items), then had both the front and rear discs drilled and chamfered to save about 21 pounds per wheel in unsprung weight. This is a step requiring the services of a good machine shop or an outfit like Racecrafters where we had ours done. If the price of $40 per disc seems high, consider the facts that the operation is very time-consuming and that the hardened steel discs require the use of ultra-high-carbon cutting tools.

Koni shocks are fitted at the rear, but, once more, we went a step beyond the norm. The Koni housings were replaced with Wheelsmith Engineering's $40 aluminum housings that are being used on so many motocrossers these days. 110cc of Bel Ray 300 shock oil in each is just the ticket. We weren't after an oil cooling advantage with this change; it was simply for cosmetics. Wheelsmith charges $10 extra to install the Konis into their housings. S&W 75-lb. springs complete the shock picture at the rear.

Morris Industries' aluminum wheels are probably the strongest anywhere, as can be attested to by the fact that many of the top factory road racers are using them. Elliot Morris is a perfectionist and it really shows in his finished product. The production rims are centrifugally cast in aluminum alloy and are 100 percent penetrant-inspected. They're available in a natural finish, or black anodized with hi-lite polish. Specs are purely to aircraft standards. All kits, whether they be in the 16, 18 or 19-inch size, come with bearing hub adapters and spacers. The standard Yamaha front disc carrier bolted right to the front wheel.

The trick-looking aluminum sprocket is from Circle Industries and is a special cush drive unit. The cush drive greatly reduces wear in the drive train, especially the transmission. The sprockets come with several lightening holes, but we added more, chamfered the edges and painted the insides of the holes blue to accentuate the appearance. With three more teeth on the rear sprocket and the larger tire on the rear, we approximated the same overall gearing as stock. Drag racing or quicker acceleration would require a 14-tooth sprocket on the engine rather than the stock 15-toother.

The torque arm is a specially fabricated unit that you can duplicate in your garage or at the machine shop at your local adult education facility.

The biggest problem we faced on the entire machine was finding a master cylinder. The magnesium Lockspeed systems from England are probably the best, but nobody has any. Brad Stanley of Speed & Research said he could solve our problem by mounting a Girling sports car master cylinder similar to that he was using on his road racer. Sure enough, after a few brief tests, the system worked perfectly.

Brad machined the housing and the installation ended up being a snap. The reservoir was custom-made and mounted directly to the master cylinder. Brad may have started a big trend with the disc brake guys. The price of the master cylinder is about $30 and the reservoir is $18.50 from Speed & Research. They were also the ones who fabricated the stainless steel braided brake lines. Kits are available for most Yamahas for $19.95.

Tires are extremely critical on a machine of this type and we pondered several before we made our choice. Our

A Step Further

timing was just right to get our hands on a new set of Goodyear prototypes we had been waiting to try for some time. They will be available for sale by the time you read this. Fitted at the front is an MJ90 3:25-19 raised-white-letter job that retails for about $40. The rear is an MN90 4:00-18 that sells for about $50. Tread pattern was developed from racing and is the same compound as the famous Goodyear D/T rubber used on the National dirt track racing circuit. The tires on *de Cafito* are the same as the ones used on Yvon DuHamel's winning production class Z1 Kawasaki.

The new Goodyears are "low profile" in design with a 90 percent aspect ratio, which represents the height of the tire versus the width of the rim. Most tires have a 100 percent aspect ratio so you can see what is meant by low profile. Though it's too early for us to comment on tire wear, we can comment on road holding and overall tire feel. Looks as though the new Goodyears are going to be the hot set-up for the cafe crowd. They not only look superb, they work wonderfully. Goodyear has the answer with this one.

ENGINE

Our goal was to substantially increase the power over a usable powerband without hurting reliability or street worthiness. There is nothing worse than a machine that breaks down in rush hour traffic or that won't start just because the owner wanted better performance. We wanted none of that stuff. Yamaha had already given us an excellent start with an engine that is a performance rocket. It's a good example of how racing heritage improves the breed. Over the past five years, Yamaha 250 and 350 production racers have been the standard mount for amateur road racers the world over—professionals too. The street equivalents share many similar

features. Perhaps this is one of the most impressive things about Yamaha as a manufacturer; they are deeply involved with the racing aspects of motorcycling and are usually the first ones to innovate racing improvements into their standard production motorcycles.

As far as the 350s go, there are many similarities between the RD street bike and the TD series road racers. Absent on our machine is a wet clutch; gear ratios are spaced for street riding...but you'd be amazed at how close the engines are.

Our engine was prepared by Gene Schroeder and Jeff Cowan of Fairway Performance Products. Modifications are briefly described as follows: The heads were turned on a lathe and cc'ed, and the compression ratio was brought up to 8.0 to 1, corrected. We removed 0.072 in. from one head and 0.080 in. from the other. The angle of the squish band was recut to 17 degrees to allow a 0.050-in. deck clearance. We substituted a pair of Champion L57-R plugs for the standard ones.

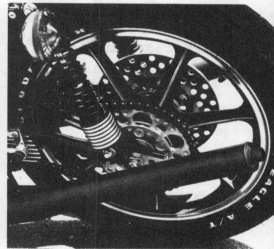

The piston modifications were made to increase rpm and horsepower, but they definitely are not a longevity item. The intake timing was increased (Poor Richard defines as: "more gas per rev"), to supercharge the incoming fuel charge via cutting the piston skirt on the intake side of the piston at the top of the intake holes. The holes are extended straight down; however, the reinforcing ribs in the piston must remain.

The crank assembly modifications are for the Sunday racer in the production and cafe racer classes. A road racer crank assembly was substituted, not for increased ponies, but for reliability during those extended nine grand tach readings. This little swap over gets expensive. It involves two road racing rod kits, which include roller bearings (as opposed to ball bearings), to handle heavier loads, a slotted rod to increase the oil feed to the crank for more life under high rpm and finally those neato silver-plated titanium bearing cages that add that all important pizazz.

MAJOR COMPONENT WEIGHT CHART
1974 YAMAHA RD350

Starting Dry Weight 339   Completed Weight 308
  Front 143 = 42.2 percent   Front 143 = 46.5 percent
  Rear 196 = 57.8 percent   Rear 165 = 53.5 percent

COMPONENT	ORIGINAL WT. IN LB.	FINAL WT.	DIFFERENCE
Complete front wheel assy.	23.50	26.0	2.50
Front fender (inc. brackets)	4.0	1:25	2.75
Handlebars	2.25	1.25	0.50
Mirrors	0.50	0.75	0.25
Tank	7.25	5.75	1.50
Seat	8.75	4.50	4.25
Fender/tail piece assy. (inc. taillight)	8.50	5.50	3.0
Shocks and springs	6.50	6.50	0
Exhaust system (pair)	17.0	12.50	4.50
Front foot peg assy.	5.0	0	5.0
Rear centerstand assy.	3.25	0	3.25
Rear wheel (complete)	36.50	35.0	1.50
Chain guide	1.25	0	1.25
Fairing assy. (with brackets)	0	7.75	7.75
Swinging arm	6.50	6.50	0
Miscellaneous	14.25	0	14.25
		Total Difference	31

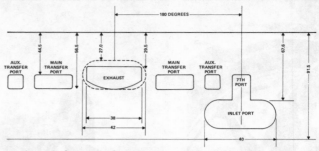

Porting diagram shows before and after cylinder modifications performed by Fairway. The important thing is to shape the exhaust ports correctly so they won't swallow the Dykes rings.

A Step Further

The crank was disassembled, the new parts substituted, reassembled and trued to within less than 0.0005 in...and that's close! This tight tolerance greatly helps reduce vibration and horsepower loss at high rpm.

Our inner and outer clutch hubs were drilled out to save a few ounces and dazzle any onlookers who might observe our disassembled engine. The cylinder porting basically involves raising the exhaust port to 27mm from the stock 29.5mm, widening the exhaust to 42mm and matching the transfer ports. The key to the whole thing is in shaping the exhaust port correctly so that the ports don't swallow the Dykes rings.

Being great believers in reducing friction, we contacted the Kal-Gard people and they convinced us that we should try coating the engine internals with Kal-Gard. They claim a 10 percent increase in horsepower and a substantial lowering of the transmission oil temperature. We figured that since it must run cooler and slipperier with Kal-Gard, we would put less oil of a thinner type in the trans. So far, so good.

To improve the breathing efficiency, we installed a K&N air filter. Don't try to install any air filters directly onto the carburetors. The only way to go is to keep the still air box and replace the stock filter.

Many hours were spent on the dyno developing an exhaust system that would develop more horsepower over a broader powerband than the stock system and still be as quiet. We tested several of the leading expansion chambers on the market, and, interestingly enough, only one was better than stock

LIST OF SUPPLIERS

1. Wheelsmith Engineering
   3635 W. McFadden
   Santa Ana, CA 92704
   (714) 839-0150

2. J&R Expansion Chambers
   1967 Glassell St.
   Orange, CA 92667
   (714) 998-6410

3. Racecrafters International
   7916 Sunset Blvd.
   Hollywood, CA 90046
   (213) 876-3600 (catalog $1.00)

4. Fairway Racing Products
   1350 E. Yorba Linda Blvd.
   Placentia, CA 92670
   (714) 524-1205

5. Kal-Gard
   7118 Gerald Ave.
   Van Nuys, CA 91406
   (213) 997-1673

6. Dick's Cycle West
   304 Agostino
   San Gabriel, CA 91776
   (213) 287-9656 (catalog $2.00)

7. Morris Industries
   3853 S. Main St.
   Santa Ana, CA 92707
   (714) 540-5206

8. General Engineered Products
   17332 Irvine Blvd., Unit N
   Tustin, CA 92680
   (714) 990-0775 (catalog $1.00)

9. K&N Engineering
   P.O. Box 1329
   Riverside, CA 92502
   (714) 682-8813

10. Circle Industries
    17901 E. Arenth
    City of Industry, CA 91746
    (213) 965-1622 (catalog $1.00)

11. Custom Paint Work
    581 S. Walnut
    La Habra, CA 90631
    (213) 694-4164

12. Number One Products
    11509 Bexley Drive
    Whittier, CA 90606

13. Speed & Research
    501 W. Maple, Unit L
    Orange, CA 92668
    (714) 633-9323

14. Cycle Craft
    1572 Soquel Drive
    Santa Cruz, CA 95060
    (408) 476-4566

Yamaha pipes. Obviously, Yamaha units are extremely well designed...making our job really tough.

Chuck Kayser, of J&R Expansion Chambers, worked hard on the project and came up with a pretty good answer. The first set worked well from 5500 rpm on up, but they lost five hp right at 5000 rpm, creating a flat spot smack dab in the middle of the power curve. Chuck then modified the rear cone and picked up four of that lost five horsepower, and gained everywhere else in the process. We used a rear wheel dyno and obtained a steady progression of a four-hp increase over stock at 6000 rpm up to a 10-hp increase at 8000 rpm. The J&R pipe revved to 9000, or about 1000 rpm higher than stock.

This is basically a simple change, consisting of merely bolting on a set of pipes for an increase of about 23 percent in horsepower. The powerband also becomes higher and wider. Normal installation involves cutting off your RD350 head pipe about two inches and bolting the J&R units on. Everything

fits as it should, but ground clearance seems to suffer a bit. *de Cafito* drags the ground too early at present, and we weren't able to solve the problem before this issue went to press. The right pipe drags, as does the left when the sidestand is removed, so we've still got some work ahead of us. After all, handling is a great big part of cafe racing, and making sparks on the pavement with your pipes just doesn't get it...especially when the pipes set you back $80 or $90, depending on whether they're chrome or flat black.

COSTS

To give you an idea of what some of these modifications cost, we'll give you Fairway's charges for their services. Other dealers or shops will probably vary. That's why it's always a good idea to shop around and determine who can do the best job for you. Talking to customers in and around the shop is another way to insure yourself that the place is reputable. Here's how Fairway works it.

Photography: Barry Watkins, Fernando Belair

```
Curb weight (w/half-tank fuel), lb. . . . . . . . . . . . . . . . . . 336
Weight bias, front/rear, percent . . . . . . . . . . . . . . . . . . . 47/53
Total brake swept area, sq. in. . . . . . . . . . . . . . . . . . . . 229
Brake loading, lb./sq. in. (160 lb. rider) . . . . . . . . . . . . . . 2.16
Braking distance:
   from 30 mph, ft. . . . . . . . . . . . . . . . . . . . . . . . . . . 31
   from 60 mph, ft. . . . . . . . . . . . . . . . . . . . . . . . . . . 123
Standing one quarter mile, sec. . . . . . . . . . . . . . . . . . . 14.05
   terminal speed, mph . . . . . . . . . . . . . . . . . . . . . . . 93.07
Top speed (actual @ 8500 rpm), mph . . . . . . . . . . . . . . . 100
```

COMPONENT COST ANALYSIS

ITEM	APPROX. COST
Morris front wheel (inc. finish and bearing adapters)	$160
Racecrafter front and rear disc drilling service	80
Goodyear MJ90 3.25-19 front tire	40
Fork machine work	10 (est.)
Number One Products trick fork kit	10
Dick's Cycle West front fender	15
Dick's Cycle West fairing	155
General Engineered Products tank	100
General Engineered Products seat and tail piece combination	135
Koni Shocks	60
Wheelsmith aluminum housings	40
S&W rear springs	12
Taillight	6
Morris rear mag (inc. finish and bearing adapters)	170
Circle Industries sprocket and cushion drive kit	30
Yamaha disc and carrier for the rear wheel	40
Yamaha caliper assy.	75
Speed & Research master cylinder and reservoir	49
Speed & Research front and rear braided brake lines	40
Custom Paint Work paint job	115
Ronnie Lyster pin-stripe job	30
K&N air filter	6
Lettering	50
General Engineered Products rear-sets	70
Rear view mirrors (pair)	7
TOTAL TO HERE	**$1533**

PERFORMANCE MODIFICATIONS

Fairway Racing Products total performance package (inc. exhaust system)	270
TOTAL	**$1803**

NOTE: These prices are approximate and apply to the time of construction of our project machine. It is quite likely that most of them have increased slightly since the date we went to press.

If you want the whole shootin' match they need your crank assembly, both heads, both barrels and pistons, and will ship you the high performance package for $200. Prices separately are:

1. Racing crank assembly service $36, plus two rod kits at $24 each and two roller bearings at $16 each. Total crank service is $116.

2. The best performance buy in the engine itself is the $90 special that includes porting both cylinders and modifying the heads and pistons. This is the recommended budgeteer plan to dazzle the speed freaks.

3. You can get the J&R pipes for $79.95 in black or for $10 more get chrome. Chrome is for sissy cafe racers, however; flat black is in.

4. The drilled inner and outer clutch hub costs $12.50 exchange.

Finishing off *de Cafito* is Porsche acrylic lacquer from their 1974 color list. We used Marathon blue, a good solid color with pin-striped highlighting. Clear bullet-proof epoxy was added to help protect the finish from fuel damage and possible chipping. Ronnie Lyster, a well known pin-striper in Southern California, put his talents to good use on the RD Project bike.

Here are some hints to ease your mind financially with the project. Remember that many of the items can be removed if you sell your bike and can be sold for a reasonable percentage of their original cost. Or, you can transfer them to your next machine, perhaps with only minor modifications.

Many people won't be willing to pay what you feel the accessories are worth when they are on a machine for sale, so put as much of it back in original condition as possible, and then sell your bike.

On the other hand, if you need immediate financial assistance to buy an accessory, there are many parts readily saleable on your stock RD. For instance, any RD250 owner would be wise to buy your front wheel to convert to a disc brake. There are other similar examples.

It takes quite a while to build a machine such as this. Be patient and do a good job. Our machine took about seven months, but much of that was spent waiting for accessories to be designed and marketed.

A motorcycle is a compromise—none is perfect in all realms. Traits are juggled and traded off to obtain those desirable factors.

There is a great paradox in the motorcycle field. In road racing the Japanese easily dominate almost all major racing events (with the possible exception of MV Augusta in Europe). The Japanese have the most street-like street bikes and the most race-worthy race bikes, but they offer practically nothing in-between.

A few machines like the RD350 hint at sport, but nothing from Japan really is comparable to the European machines like the Ducati Desmo Sport and Moto Guzzi Sport. The European road racing motorcycles rarely place high in the standings of road race events, yet their sport offerings are about the only cafe racers on the market. We attempted to bridge the gap between the pure street bike and the pure road racer.

Cafe racers we've observed come in two general categories. The first group is modified for cosmetic appeal. The stock tank, seat, fenders, handlebars and foot controls are replaced with the latest high-fashion equipment. The second group normally includes most of the above modifications, but the machine is further refined for a higher level of handling and performance. These modifications consist of high-performance tires, improved shocks, lighter components—including alloy wheels—tanks, fairings, beefed-up swinging arms, high-performance exhaust systems, disc brakes, etc.

Our project attempted to incorporate both of the above. And, we included an explanation of the parts involved so that you could either duplicate this machine or parts of it, depending on whether you prefer performance or appearance.

Cafe racers are really starting to come into their own and, hopefully soon, we'll see an exciting new era in motorcycling, thanks to machines such as *de Cafito*.

Cycle World Road Test

YAMAHA XS650B

Line Leadership At Yamaha Belongs To The 650 . . . A Tall Order For A Vertical Twin

■ WHEN OTHER manufacturers are dazzling the motorcycle world with innovative new models and displays of R&D genius in their top-of-the-line equipment, Yamaha seems content to rest on its laurels...or at least on the steadfast solidarity and age-old appeal of the 650 Vertical Twin. Displacing the never-weaned 750 Twin from the head of the Yamaha pack, the OHC 650 goes up against stiff competition with practical, but non-earthshaking credentials.

It's the traditional British concept in a far more refined and civilized, yet still incomplete package, despite six years of fussing. That's what we said...six years. Seems almost like yesterday that the 1970 green and white, XS1 was introduced; the bike with the right idea but a long way to go. And it's gone a long way; on to the XS1B, the XS2, the TX650 and TX650A...to now, the XS650B. But there's been a whole lot more going down than mere alphabet changes. One ride gives more than subtle indication that the XS650B is a vastly improved and different motorcycle than the original XS1.

But even the original was lauded as the Twin to end traditional British woes. No more oil leaks they said. No more electrical problems they promised. Quieter was the word. "Numbing vibrations cut drastically," read the bold type. And even the promise of push-button starting. Hark! A Beezer-Trump minus the acne. But it was not to be.

Though the XS1 followed through and delivered many of those expected promises, it lacked an all-important ingredient, the type you cannot put your finger on. Distress came to many when they found that the XS1 felt *Japanese*. So what's wrong with a Japanese motorcycle feeling Japanese? Everything...when it's supposed to feel British.

After years of Triumph and BSA Twins, riders were *ingrained* with the idea that the Britains had themselves a couple of motorcycles that handled beautifully. That they did. For many riders that feature alone (coupled with good engine performance), outweighed the hassles then inherent in a British piece of equipment. Conversely, all the goodies and conveniences found on Yamaha's new 650 *did not* outweigh the fact that it steered like a wheelbarrow and could be

Photography: Bob Atkinson, D. Randy Riggs

downright treacherous in certain situations. So in the period of time from then to now, Yamaha has gone to work on its 650 to correct the imperfections, while the British have teetered on the edge of doom, beset with labor problems. Yamaha has succeeded in clearing up many of its; the British are still struggling.

The XS2B of 1975 is virtually a carbon copy of last year's TX650A...with some new paint. Significant changes had taken place in the '73/'74 models and Yamaha was apparently satisfied with the results, hence the lack of giant upheavals in the present model.

Smoothness is now a touted feature of many machines in the industry. Yamaha felt the trait important enough to warrant complex contrarotating weights and balancers in their 500 and 750 Twins. The 500 has been successful, the 750 not. And in the meantime, Yamaha was bugged with a 650 that shook...more than noticeably. So with all this emphasis on smoothness and consumer awareness (from reading motorcycle magazines), they went to work on the problem in the simplest terms possible. This meant curing what they had, thus not entailing a major redesign or engineering blast.

Compression ratios were lowered, then raised. Nothing too significant happened. Pistons were then lightened 20 percent to reduce the reciprocating mass inside the engine. Add to this lighter connecting rods, and things start falling into place. The 650 was smoother.

Most motorcycle enthusiasts realize that this 650 vertical

Twin is much more than just another engine to Yamaha. It was and is their legal connection to AMA professional dirt track racing, their basis for the power unit in the machines run by National Champ Ken Roberts, who twice has given Yamaha that Number One plate. And that single digit number is worth much in terms of sales, not just of 650s, but of everything in the Yamaha line-up. Number One means exposure and plenty of free advertising. And this is the motor that got them there, though the differences in Roberts' engine and the unit in a standard XS2B are equatable to those between an armadillo and a tiger.

Like a British Twin, the engine is compact, simple and straight forward. Unlike older Triumphs and BSAs, oil leaks are minimal, but the latest Triumphs are much better in that respect as well, so that advantage is of lesser significance. There are no pushrods to operate the valves, rather a simpler and more efficient single overhead camshaft. The cam gets its drive from a single-row chain running from the center of the crankshaft. Chain tension is maintained by an idler gear located behind the cylinder.

Professional racers switching from Triumphs to Yamahas often have problems getting used to the Yamaha's quick-to-rev-and-unrev type of power delivery. Gene Romero, factory team rider, relates the feeling back to 1965 and his 500 Triumphs. "You gotta keep 'em revving off the corners or they'll bog just like the old 500s. This is due to the small size of the Yamaha flywheels, and this quick revving ability is

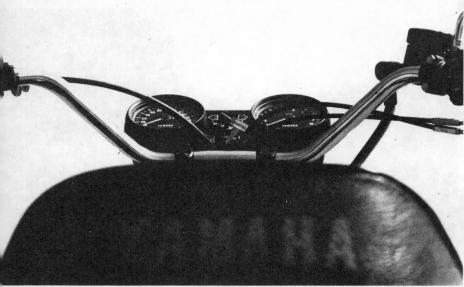

immediately apparent in the stock machine as well as the racing equipment. Sitting at standstill and blipping the throttle gets an immediate reaction from the engine. And the lack of flywheel effect lets the rider know in an instant if he has selected too high a gear in a particular situation. The 650 will buck and stumble until the rider gets wise.

Common practice on many bikes is a pressed-together crankshaft assembly, and the 650 Yamaha follows suit. Four full-circle crank wheels are employed and the center shaft and wheels are splined to prevent the movement or variance of these parts. Three roller bearings and a ball bearing support the crank assembly. Few problems have ever beset this area so we know they're robust enough. The lighter connecting rods turn on needle bearings. A 360-degree crank configuration means that the pistons travel up and down together; the rump, rump, rump of the exhaust gives that away in an instant.

Straight cut gears hook up the crank and mainshaft of the five-speed transmission. Straight-cut gears are noisy but efficient, neither of which is apparent to the rider of the 650.

A medium to hard tug on the clutch handle operates the five metal and six cork-lined friction plates of the wet clutch assembly. Six springs provide the tension to hold the plates in position. The clutch hub bushing is lubricated by pressurized oil from the mainshaft.

Shifting our particular test machine was a bit peculiar. It seemed as though the rider had to force the gears into position; not that it caused missed shifts or problems such as

YAMAHA

that...it was just disconcerting to put so much pressure on the gear-change lever. Lever travel, by the way, is short. Coupled with the boot pressure necessary for clean shifts, it made the gearbox feel vague. At times neutral was evasive as well. Much of the time we resorted to finding the "N" quadrant when rolling to a stop. Far easier that way. Ratios are well matched to the engine and allow good acceleration as well as sufficient top speed.

The recommended 20/50-wt. engine oil is delivered by a trochoidal pump (rotary type) to the main bearings, crank pins, transmission main shaft, clutch bushing, shifter fork guide bar and rocker arms. The remainder of the engine parts are lubricated by "oil splash." A convenient dip stick lets the rider keep tabs on oil level.

Conventional and usually reliable battery ignition is used on the S. Two sets of points, located on the upper left of the cylinder head, trigger the secondary coils at the prescribed time and furnish spark for the plugs. The points are fitted directly to the camshaft. An advance mechanism is used to retard the timing for easy starting and smooth idle. Yamaha dropped the previously used compression release from the 650 when they discovered that it wasn't necessary to allow the hefty starter motor to spin the engine over. Works just fine without it, thanks.